Cookbook for Young Chefs

The First Friendly Cookbook of
Step by Step Recipes
at Your Children

75 recipes+10 bonus!

Table of Contents

Introduction

Are you tired of constantly giving your kids sugary and unhealthy meals? Do you not know how to teach your children the basics of the kitchen? Do you want to have enjoyable moments with the family? Then this cookbook might be able to solve all your problems.

Many parents don't know how to interact with their kids. They don't know how to make them learn important skills and utilize their creativity and curiosity. It's fine if you're one of those parents. Whether one is a new or old parent, everyone encounters difficulty in raising their kids. You gradually learn the best ways to handle your children, and this comes with many years of experience. The important thing is that you are looking to find solutions and want to do the best for your child.

Even though you are well intended, children of all ages try to resist your teachings and run away from work. Whether your child is six or sixteen, they will always find excuses not to learn to cook. Fast food joints can hold the blame, but they are not the only problem. The home dishes we make look complex; many take hours to make and require a particular set of skills. You need to make cooking fun to them so they, happily, join you in your kitchen. They will grow up without fearing ingredients and never live on just pasta and bread when they are on their own. They will gain confidence and increase their ability to connect with others.

If you want the best for your kids, you need to introduce them in the kitchen as soon as their motor skills activate. You'll be surprised by what little kids can do! If you give them the opportunity, they will not only live up to your expectations, but they will exceed them.

Now, you might wonder, "Where can I find healthy recipes that my kids can easily make?» No need to look any further. This book has all the knowledge that your child needs to start their steps in the kitchen. In this book, more than 70 recipes have been provided which are highly nutritious and also very easy to make in a few minutes.

Nowadays, you will see that many products targeted at children are usually sugary treats and chips. Children are not generally good at understanding the harmful effects of these treats, and they usually make them feel fat and sluggish. We can't blame them for making the wrong choice, but we can tell them what healthy options are and show them that they can be as delicious as other products in the candy store.

This book provides recipes that are low in calories, low in cholesterol, and do not contain any harmful ingredients. You can be assured of your child's health when you give them these recipes to try.

You might wonder why I am so passionate about teaching kids how to cook. I am a Mom and possess many years of experience with other Moms who only had one thought in mind: How to raise their kids the best they can. This thought led to many ideas, including meals for kids. These recipes are a collection of my tested recipes from my cookbook. No matter who you are, a grandpa, a scout teacher, or a teenager yourself, you will find these recipes a joy to make and eat. My mission is to provide as much help as I can to all the children and their guardians.

You will be surprised by the results of this activity. Cooking involves skill-based tasks that everyone should learn. It teaches children how to read and follow instructions properly, as it enhances their ability to understand the material. All the measuring cups and teaspoons will make them accustomed to numbers and simple calculations. They will learn how to handle and use different veggies, fruits, and learn even more about ingredients. It is a way to utilize their young energy to create something productive that will assist them later in life. They might grow up to become experts in the kitchen because you introduced them to it in such a fun and creative way. Most importantly, you will make great memories together, and your children will always remember and thank you for what you taught them.

My friends and their children together have tried the recipes in this book. The kids always are so happy, and I am constantly receiving thanks from my girlfriends and sweet, heartwarming letters from their children. They thank me and tell me how delicious the meals were. I can guarantee that once you start cooking with your kids, they will be much happier than before.

So, now you know the benefits of cooking with your kids and teaching them the skills of the kitchen. Knowledge is useless if you don't apply it in your life. If your kid is more than 6 years old and can comfortably move around the house and play all day, then they are fine in the kitchen. With you by their side, they will start to learn to make these easy recipes, and in time, will begin to prepare them without you around. It will become a massive time saver. Don't sleep on this great idea. If you don't take action now, you might miss this amazing opportunity to help your kids. Start cooking with them today and reap the benefits.

The recipes in this book are classified for your ease. They are separated into breakfast, lunch, dinner, snacks, and desserts. You will also find kitchen safety instructions for your little ones. Keep on reading this book to uncover all these secrets and more.

Dear reader, visit my author page to know what books I am writing to you. I will be pleased if you add a review and tell me what recipes you want to see more of.

It is very interesting for me to write a book with you! I'm waiting for you on my author page.
https://www.amazon.com/-/e/B08LVV4NC7

Chapter1: Rules of Safe Behavior in the Kitchen

Cooking is a fun and exciting journey. You mix, play, and in the end, you have a treat to enjoy. However, this activity can turn into a disaster if you do not keep safety precautions in mind. It is especially important when children are involved. Safety should always be the first thing on your mind as a parent. There are many ways for you and your child to get injured if you are not careful about them.

The kitchen contains many objects that can be dangerous, and you need to be aware of environmental hazards as well. Some equipment and utensils have sharp edges, like knives, some equipment run on electricity like a toaster, and some equipment deal with heat and fire like the oven and stove. The kitchen is filled with leftovers and pieces of food that can promote the build-up of bacteria. Being aware of safety is a habit that you should develop in yourself, as well as in your children.

Instructions for kids

Thoroughly read the entire recipe, so you know what you are doing

Never use the stove and oven alone. Heat and flames can hurt you, so you have to be extra careful around them.

Wash your hands before and after you are done with cooking. Use soap, and dry your hands after you clean.

Put on an apron. Wipe your hands on the apron when they get dirty. If they are too dirty, then wash them.

Clear and clean repeatedly. Don't make a mess in the kitchen. Throw something away immediately, and after you finish, clean the counter.

Use the knife properly. It would be best if you use the proper technique when you use the knife.

You choose a knife that is not too big in your hand. You should feel comfortable doing this.

Grasp the handle tightly. Hold the cutting edge of the blade down. Place your index finger on the full side of the blade.

Start cutting in constant motion with no distractions. Place the food lengthwise on the cutting board and push the blade away from you. Grip the food by your left hand, with your fingers tucked inwards.

Instructions for adults

The most important thing in the kitchen is always to be aware of what you do. Pay full attention to the task at hand, and do not multitask. Doing so will minimize injuries in the kitchen. One little slip can lead to a very bad outcome.

Always have all your equipment near you or fully prepared when you make a meal beforehand. Looking for something haphazardly while cooking the recipe may cause an accident.

Before doing a step, like cutting, always plan on how to clean it. Always prepare a garbage bag or bin near your cutting board so that you can immediately throw away the skins and unwanted bits and pieces. If you are using a utensil, place the used ones separate from the other, and clean them immediately as well.

Have important safety equipment near you, like gloves, oven mitts, paper towels, etcetera. You will always be prepared and never forget to use them when needed in a rush.

Constantly wash your hands. You are using different ingredients and touching all types of surfaces and equipment. The food needs to be as clean as possible, and to ensure that, you must clean your hands often.

Be aware of people in the kitchen. Do not bump into one another or accidentally hurt them. (Be extra aware of kids, as they like to move around a lot).

Place knives and other sharp utensils, which should NOT be in reach of children, in a locked or high up drawer.

Do not use metal or heatproof bowls for microwaving. They will also get very hot. Do not even use aluminium foil inside a microwave.

Learn how to use a knife properly. Bad technique can lead to cuts and bleeding. Use a dull knife when children are around.

Be careful about handling hot objects, especially hot liquid. Use gloves and never be in a rush.

Don't wear anything loose, and this includes long loose sleeves, no dangling jewellery, no open long hair, etcetera. These are a fire hazard. Also, make sure to tie your and your child's hair to prevent it from going into food as well.

When you use a pot, make sure the handles do not face yourself or your child. They should always face the opposite side. Also, keep potholders away from flames.

If you spill something, clean it up immediately. Not only bacteria start to develop, but there can be more chances of you or your child slipping.

Do not let food sit in the kitchen that may spoil. Meat and dairy can spoil quickly. They leave a bad smell along with attracting insects. Always put them in the refrigerator when you are not using them.

Separate all the types of meat and store them in separate containers or boxes. Not doing so can lead to cross-contamination and food poisoning.

Get a fire extinguisher and learn how to use it. Sometimes, flames get out of control, and you need to be fully prepared for such a situation.

Chapter 2: How to Use the Recipes?

Hurray, we are starting to cook. First, wash your hands and put on your aprons. To make everything easy and simple, I will explain to you how to use the recipes.

Block1:

This will show you the picture of the dish and how the meal will look like after you have prepared it. It will also give you a plating idea, but you can plate your dish however you like.

Block 2:

The recipes will be classified into three levels according to complexity. They are mentioned in the form of levels at the beginning of the recipe with «Level 1» being easy, «Level 2» as a little more complex or rare, and «Level 3» as the hardest.

Each recipe also comes with an estimated Cooking Time and Total Cooking Time. Cooking Time tells you how much time is needed to prepare the dish. It tells you, roughly, how long you will be in the kitchen. Total Cooking Time tells you how long it is going to take to finish the dish. If you leave a dish to cool in the fridge or to cook in the oven, your Cooking Time will be lesser than Total Cooking Time.

Before each recipe, the Number of Ingredients is mentioned. This number will help you gather all your ingredients and utensils that you may need. Before you start, be sure you have everything you need near you.

The serving number tells you how many servings the recipe will make after you prepare it. It tells you how many people can eat the dish at the end.

Block3:

This will show the Ingredients List. It will be written in a list form. It will tell you all the ingredients that you need written side by side their quantities required by the recipe. Use this information to gather everything from different parts of the kitchen and place them near you.

Block 4:

This will tell you the Cooking Recipe. The information is presented in a list form. You will follow each step one by one to get to the result. Finish the first step before moving on to the other.

Block5:

This will tell you the Energy Value of the recipe. Food has all types of nutrients in it; we must know how much goes into our body. Eating too much or too little of a nutrien can prove harmful. Nutrients provide energy, and we should know their amounts like carbohydrates, fats, and protein. Other nutrients do not provide energy but are equally important such as fiber and sodium.

Calories: Everybody needs the energy to live, and we need a certain amount of it every day. Calories tell you how much total energy is stored in the food in the form of fats, carbohydrates, and proteins.

Carbohydrate: This is a nutrient that gives you energy. Simple carbohydrates come from fruits/vegetables and sugar. There are complex carbohydrates that come from starchy vegetables and whole grains. They come from foods like beans, legumes, groats, flour, potatoes, other vegetables, and leafy greens. Complex carbohydrates also include fiber. Fiber is essential for digestion and helps you feel full after a meal.

Protein: It is an important nutrient for growth. Protein builds the muscles, organs, and repairs your wounds. It is present in eggs, lentils, meat, and etcetera.

Fats: They are energy-packed nutrients that are important for development and growth. There are two types of fats. Healthy fats or good fats come from seafood, vegetable oil, nuts, and avocado. They have essential fatty acids and Vitamin E. Unhealthy fats or bad fats are a part of animal products such as meats and dairy. Fats should not be consumed in excess.

Sodium: It is one of the most important minerals that help regulate good water levels and help our muscles and nerves to function properly. They are essential, but they should not be eaten too much. In excess amounts, it can cause high blood pressure and related diseases.

Eggs – Eggs are versatile in their use and loved by almost everyone. They are nutritious sources of protein which are needed for kids to grow big and strong.

Whole-milk – Growing children need strong bones to grow healthy. Whole milk provides a great source of calcium, which will do just that. It also has other nutrients that help more calcium enter in our body.

Whole-grain cereal – Whole grains help curb that big appetite without making you gain weight. It is low in calories and ensures that you do not get sick.

Whole-wheat flour – It is packed with minerals and vitamins and minerals. Whole-wheat flour will help your kid become smarter.

Cheese – It is filled with good protein that will help you grow big and strong. They also make you feel less hungry and more satisfied.

Greek yogurt – Yogurt is full of calcium, and they are also an excellent source of different minerals such as potassium. They all are needed for strong, growing children.

Soy milk – Soy milk is low in fat and filled with nutrition. It is not only filled with flavor but also in iron and other minerals. It will help you maintain your weight.

Avocado – This ingredient is extremely creamy and flavourful. It is a good source of iron, potassium, magnesium, and other nutrients. It will help prevent anemia from developing in kids.

Oatmeal – Oatmeal is extremely healthy. It makes you feel less hungry and is low in calories. Itey helps remove all the bad fat from your body and keep you smiling.

Banana – Bananas are versatile fruits, loved by everyone. They are packed with nutrients such as potassium, niacin, and B6 Vitamin. They help thin kids gain weight in a healthy manner.

Chia seeds – Don't run away from seeds. They are delicious and filled with minerals. This one is filled with antioxidants and Omega-3s as well. If you cannot eat dairy, then chia seeds can save the day.

Bacon – In moderate amounts, bacon gives high-quality animal protein for children to grow. It also has all the vitamin B that you cannot get from plants. Just be careful not to use too much in your dishes.

Almonds – Almonds help your brain to develop and grow. You will focus better, and perform better academically, after you have some in your breakfast.

Hard-Boiled Eggs

Yield: 4 eggs, 2 eggs per serving

Preparation Time: 15 minutes

Cooking Time: 8 minutes

Total Time: 23 minutes

Difficulty: Level 1

MAIN INGREDIENTS:

- 4 eggs, at room temperature
- 3 cups of water

DIRECTIONS

Adult + Kid:
Take a medium pot, arrange eggs in it, and then pour in water; water should be 1-inch over the top of the eggs.
Place the pot over high heat, cover it with the lid, and bring the water to boil.
Adult:
Then immediately remove the pot from heat and let the egg stand in water for 12 minutes.
Kid:
After 12 minutes, take a large bowl, fill it with chilled water, and then place the boiled eggs in it.
Let the eggs cool completely, then take them out and then peel the eggs.
Serve the eggs as you like.

Nutritional Information per Serving:

Calories: 310 Cal; Total Fat: 22 g; Saturated Fat: 6.6 g; Cholesterol: 746 mg; Carbohydrates: 2.2 g; Fiber: 0 g; Sugar: 2.2 g; Protein: 26 g;

Herb and Cheese Omelet

Yield: 1 omelet

Preparation Time: 5 minutes

Cooking Time: 5 minutes

Total Time: 10 minutes

Difficulty: Level 1

MAIN INGREDIENTS:

- 2 tablespoons chopped basil
- 1/16 teaspoon salt
- 1/16 teaspoon ground black pepper
- 1 teaspoon butter, unsalted
- 3 eggs, at room temperature
- 2 tablespoons shredded cheddar cheese

DIRECTIONS:

Adult + Kid:
Chop the basil leaves.
Kid:
Crack the eggs in a large bowl, add salt, black pepper, and basil and then whisk until combined.
Adult:
Take a large skillet pan, about 6-inch, place it over low heat, add butter, and then wait until it melts.
Tilt the pan to coat it with melted butter, pour in the egg mixture, and then stir in immediately with a rubber spatula.
Push the outer part of the cooked egg to the center, and keep doing it until the egg begins to firm up; the top of the eggs will be a bit runny, and the bottom will be cooked.
Adult + Kid:
Sprinkle cheese on top of eggs and then continue cooking the omelet for 1 to 2 minutes or until the cheese melts.
Lose the edge of the omelet with a spatula, slide it to a plate and then fold it over.
Serve immediately.

Nutritional Information per Serving:

Calories: 256 Cal; Total Fat: 18 g; Saturated Fat: 7 g; Cholesterol: 569 mg; Carbohydrates: 1 g; Fiber: 21 g; Sugar: 3 g; Protein: 21 g;

Eggs in the Hole

Yield: 4 eggs in the hole, 1 egg in the hole per serving

Preparation Time: 10 minutes

Cooking Time: 18 minutes

Total Time: 28 minutes

Difficulty: Level 1

MAIN INGREDIENTS:

- 8 slices of whole wheat bread
- 4 slices of bacon
- ¼ teaspoon salt
- 1 tablespoon butter, unsalted
- ¼ teaspoon ground black pepper
- 4 eggs, at room temperature

DIRECTIONS:

Adult:
 Take a large skillet pan, place it over medium-high heat and then let it heat for 3 minutes.

Adult + Kid:
 Add bacon and then cook it for 3 to 4 minutes per side until golden brown and crisp.
 Then prepare the plate lined with a paper towel, place fried bacon slices on it using a tong and let it rest until required.

Kid:
 Prepare the bread and for this, cut a piece from each bread slice from the center, and use any 2 ½-inch cookie cutter like round, heart, or star.
 Add butter to the pan, let it melt, and then brush this mixture on bread slices and cut out pieces.

Adult + Kid:
 Transfer two slices into the pan with their cut-outs and then cook for 1 minute per side until nicely browned.

Adult:
 Crack the egg into each hole of the bread slice, cook for 2 minutes and then carefully flip the slice and cut out pieces.

Adult + Kid:
 Season each egg with 1/16 teaspoon of salt and black pepper and continue cooking the eggs for another 2 minutes until egg yolks are runny.
 Transfer eggs in the holes to the plates and then repeat with the remaining eggs and bread slices.
 Serve each egg in the hole with two slices of bacon.

Nutritional Information per Serving:

Calories: 244 Cal; Total Fat: 16.5 g; Saturated Fat: 3.5 g; Cholesterol: 196 mg;Carbohydrates:14.5 g;Fiber: 1. g; Sugar: 2.3 g; Protein: 9 g;

Egg Salad Sandwiches

Yield: 6 sandwiches, 1 sandwich per serving

Preparation Time: 10 minutes

Cooking Time: minutes

Total Time: 10 minutes

Difficulty: Level 1
Age range: 8 – 18 years old

MAIN INGREDIENTS:

- 12 eggs, hard-boiled, peeled
- 2 green onions, chopped
- 12 slices of whole-wheat bread
- ¼ teaspoon salt
- ¼ teaspoon ground black pepper
- 4 tablespoons butter, unsalted
- ½ cup mayonnaise

DIRECTIONS:

Kid:
Place butter in a heatproof bowl and then microwave it for 15 seconds until softened.
Boil the eggs as instructed in the recipe of hard-boiled eggs.
Transfer boiled eggs into a bowl containing chilled water, let them rest for 10 minutes, and then peel them.
Cut the eggs into slices and then mash them with a fork.
Add green onion, salt, black pepper, and mayonnaise and then stir until well combined.
Assemble the first sandwich and for this, spread 2/3 tablespoon butter on each of two bread slices.
Spread 2 to 3 tablespoons of the egg mixture on top of the buttered side of one bread slice and then cover with the other bread slice, butter side down.
Assemble remaining sandwiches in the same manner and then serve.

Nutritional Information per Serving:

Calories: 262 Cal; Total Fat: 12 g; Saturated Fat: 7 g; Cholesterol: 33 mg; Carbohydrates: 25 g; Fiber: 3 g; Sugar: 3 g; Protein: 13 g;

Grilled Cheese Sandwich

Yield: 6 sandwiches, 1 sandwich per serving

Preparation Time: 10 minutes

Cooking Time: minutes

Total Time: 10 minutes

Difficulty: Level 1

MAIN INGREDIENTS:

- 4 slices of cheddar cheese
- 8 tablespoons butter, unsalted
- 8 slices of whole-wheat bread

DIRECTIONS:

Kid:

Place butter in a heatproof bowl and then microwave it for 15 seconds until softened.

Spread ½ tablespoon butter on one side of each bread slice.

Adult:

Place a large skillet pan over medium heat and then let it heat for 2 minutes.

Then place a bread slice in it, butter-side down, place a cheese slice on it and top with another bread slice, butter-side up.

Take a heavy small pot with a flat bottom, slightly larger than the cheese sandwich in the pan, and then place the pot on top of the sandwich.

After 3 minutes, remove the pot from the sandwich, and then check its bottom side, which should have turned brown.

Lift the cheese sandwich, add 1 tablespoon butter, flip the sandwich and place it back into the pan.

Return the pot over the top of the sandwich and continue cooking it for 3 minutes.

After 3 minutes, the cheese should have melted, and the other side of the sandwich should have turned brown.

Transfer the cooked sandwich to a plate and then repeat with the remaining sandwiches.

When they are ready to eat, cut each sandwich in half and then serve.

Nutritional Information per Serving:

Calories: 244 Cal; Total Fat: 16.5 g; Saturated Fat: 3.5 g; Cholesterol: 196 mg; Carbohydrates: 14.5 g; Fiber: 1.1 g; Sugar: 2.3 g; Protein: 9 g;

Egg Wraps

Yield: 2 wraps, 1 wrap per serving

Preparation Time: 5 minutes

Cooking Time: 8 minutes

Total Time: 13 minutes

Difficulty: Level 1

MAIN INGREDIENTS:

- 4 slices of ham
- 1 cup spinach leaves, fresh
- 1 medium avocado
  4 eggs, at room temperature
- 1 tablespoon olive oil
- 2 tablespoons water
- 4 slices of cheddar cheese

Extra Ingredients:
- ¼ teaspoon salt
- ¼ teaspoon ground black pepper

DIRECTIONS:

Adult + Kid:
 Cut the avocado in half lengthwise, remove its pit, scoop out its flesh, and then cut the flesh into slices.
Kid:
 Crack the eggs in a medium bowl, add salt and black pepper, and then whisk until it is combined.
 Take a medium skillet pan, place it over medium-high heat, add oil and then let it heat for 2 minutes until ot.
Adult + Kid:
 Pour half of the egg mixture, rotate the pan to spread it all over the pan, and then cook it for 2 minutes until rm.
 Flip the egg, cook it for 1 minute, and then transfer the omelet to a cutting board.
 Repeat with the remaining egg mixture, and make another omelet.
Kid:
 Assemble the wrap and for this, layer one omelet with 2 slices of cheese on the center of the omelet and en layer with 2 slices of ham, ½ cup spinach, and ½ of avocado.
 Roll the egg over the filling and then create another wrap with the remaining omelet, cheese, ham, spinach, nd avocado.
 Serve immediately.

Nutritional Information per Serving:

Calories: 284 Cal; Total Fat: 15.5 g; Saturated Fat: 5 g; Cholesterol: 5 mg; Carbohydrates: 25.5 g; Fiber: 1 g; ugar: 1.5 g; Protein: 12 g;

French toast

MAIN INGREDIENTS:

- 5 slices of whole-wheat bread
- ½ teaspoon ground cinnamon
- 1/8 teaspoon salt
- 2 teaspoons honey
- 2 eggs, at room temperature
- 1 tablespoon butter, unsalted
- ½ cup whole-milk

DIRECTIONS:

Adult + Kid:
Prepare the breadsticks, and for this, remove the edges of bread slices by using a serrated knife and then cut into 1-inch sticks.
Kid:
Crack the eggs in a medium bowl, add salt, honey, and cinnamon, pour in the milk, and then whisk until combined.
Take a breadstick, dip it into the egg mixture until coated in egg, and then place it on a plate.
Repeat with the remaining breadsticks in the same manner.
Adult + Kid:
Take a medium skillet pan, place it over medium heat, add butter and let it melt.
Add breadsticks into the pan until the pan has filled, and then cook the breadsticks for 3 minutes per side, until golden brown.
When done, use a tong to transfer breadsticks to a plate and then repeat with the remaining breadsticks.
Serve hot with some more honey.

Nutritional Information per Serving:

Calories: 360 Cal; Total Fat: 14 g; Saturated Fat: 2.8 g; Cholesterol: 0 mg; Carbohydrates: 52.5 g; Fiber: 2 g; Sugar: 17.5 g; Protein: 6 g;

Egg and Bacon Breakfast

Yield: 2 sandwiches, 2 sandwiches per serving

Preparation Time: 10 minutes

Cooking Time: 18 minutes

Total Time: 28 minutes

Difficulty: Level 1

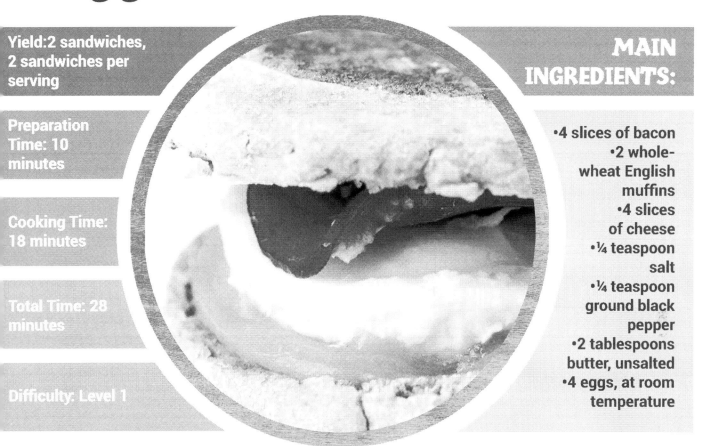

MAIN INGREDIENTS:

- 4 slices of bacon
- 2 whole-wheat English muffins
- 4 slices of cheese
- ¼ teaspoon salt
- ¼ teaspoon ground black pepper
- 2 tablespoons butter, unsalted
- 4 eggs, at room temperature

DIRECTIONS:

Adult + Kid:
 Place a frying pan over medium heat, and let it heat for 2 minutes.
 Arrange the bacon slices in the pan, and then cook them for 2 to 3 minutes per side until golden and crisp.
 When done, transfer bacon slices to a plate lined with paper towels.
Kid:
 Slice each muffin lengthwise and then toast them.
 When muffins have toast, spread ½ teaspoon butter on each half.
 Place the bottom half of the muffins on a plate. and then layer each muffin with 2 slices of cheese and 2 slices of bacon.
Adult + Kid:
 Place a large skillet pan over medium heat, add the remaining butter, and then let it melt.
 Crack the eggs into the skillet pan, sprinkle salt and black pepper over the eggs and then cook for 3 to 4 minutes until egg whites have set.
 Then carefully flip the eggs and continue cooking for 2 minutes.
 Place two eggs on top of the bacon layer, cover with the top half of the muffin, and then serve.

Nutritional Information per Serving:

Calories: 520 Cal; Total Fat: 30 g; Saturated Fat: 13 g; Cholesterol: 150 mg; Carbohydrates: 37 g; Fiber: 8 g; Sugar: 6 g; Protein: 26 g;

Quinoa, Cranberry, and Almond Granola

Yield: 12

Preparation Time: 10 minutes

Cooking Time: 50 minutes

Total Time: 60 minutes

Difficulty: Level 1

MAIN INGREDIENTS:

- 4 cups rolled oats, old-fashioned
- 1 cup dried cranberries, sweetened
- 2 cups quinoa, uncooked
- 2 cups shredded coconut, sweetened
- 1 ½ cup chopped almonds
- ½ cup roasted sunflower seeds, unsalted
- 2 ½ teaspoons vanilla extract, unsweetened

Extra Ingredients:
- 1 teaspoon ground cinnamon
- 1 cup brown sugar
- 1 teaspoon ground nutmeg
- 1/3 cup olive oil
- 1/3 cup water

DIRECTIONS:

Switch on the oven, then set it to 350 degrees F and let it preheat.

Meanwhile, pour water in a small saucepan, and add brown sugar.

Pace the pan over medium-high heat and then cook for 3 minutes until the sugar has dissolved completely and comes to a boil.

Kid:

Place oats in a large bowl, add coconut, quinoa, almonds, sunflower seeds, salt, nutmeg, and cinnamon and then stir until mixed.

Adult + Kid:

When the sugar mixture comes to a boil, whisk in vanilla and oil until well combined, and then pour the syrup over the quinoa-oats mixture.

Use a rubber spatula to mix the oat mixture and syrup until thoroughly combined.

Take a baking sheet, spoon the oat mixture in it, and then pat it with the back of a spoon until it spread in an even layer.

Adult:

Place the baking sheet into the oven and then bake the oats for 45 minutes until golden brown, stirring every 10 minutes.

When done, remove the baking sheet from the oven and let the oat mixture cool completely, stirring the mixture occasionally.

Then add cranberries into the cooled granola, transfer it to the airtight container and store it until required.

When it is ready to eat, have it straight away or serve it with yogurt.

Nutritional Information per Serving:

Calories: 583 Cal; Total Fat: 26 g; Saturated Fat: 26 g; Cholesterol: 0 mg; Carbohydrates: 76 g; Fiber: 9 g; Sugar: 33 g; Protein: 11 g;

Spinach Omelet

Yield: 1 omelet, 1 omelet per serving

Preparation Time: 5 minutes

Cooking Time: 15 minutes

Total Time: 20 minutes

Difficulty: Level 1

MAIN INGREDIENTS:

- 1 cup spinach
- 2 tablespoons chopped white onion
- 1 green chili, chopped
- ¼ teaspoon cumin seeds
- 2 teaspoons butter, unsalted
- 2 eggs, at room temperature

Extra Ingredients:

- 1/8 teaspoon salt
- 1/8 teaspoon ground black pepper

DIRECTIONS:

Kid:
Crack the eggs in a bowl and then whisk until frothy.

Adult:
Place a frying pan over medium heat, add 1 teaspoon butter, and when it melts, add cumin seeds in it.
Cook the cumin seeds until they crackle, add green chili and onion, and cook the vegetables for 3 to 5 minutes until golden brown.

Adult+ Kid:
Add chopped spinach, cook for 3 minutes until spinach leaves shrimps, and then remove the pan from heat.
Spoon the spinach mixture into the bowl containing eggs, add salt and then stir until well mixed.

Adult:
Return the frying pan over low heat, add remaining butter and let it melt.

Adult + Kid:
Pour the spinach-egg mixture into the pan, spread it evenly, sprinkle black pepper over the egg, and then cook the omelet for 4 minutes until its bottom has cooked.
Carefully flip the omelet, continue cooking it for 2 minutes, and then transfer it to a plate.
Serve straight away.

Nutritional Information per Serving:

Calories: 236 Cal; Total Fat: 17 g; Saturated Fat: 4.8 g; Cholesterol: 410 mg; Carbohydrates: 3.7 g; Fiber: 1 g; Sugar: 0.6 g; Protein: 16 g;

Yogurt with Cereal and Bananas

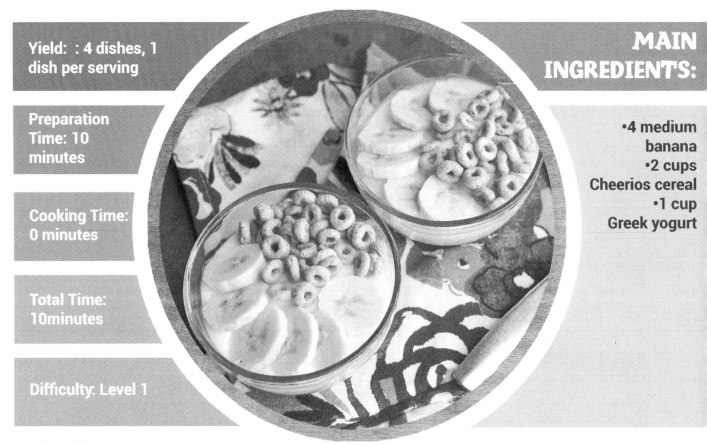

Yield: : 4 dishes, 1 dish per serving

Preparation Time: 10 minutes

Cooking Time: 0 minutes

Total Time: 10minutes

Difficulty: Level 1

MAIN INGREDIENTS:

- •4 medium banana
- •2 cups Cheerios cereal
- •1 cup Greek yogurt

DIRECTIONS:

Peel the bananas and then cut them into slices.

Take four mason jars or glass dishes and then layer its bottom with ¼ cup of yogurt.

Top the yogurt layer with ½ cup of cereal in each jar, and then layer with slices of 1 banana.

Top with the remaining yogurt, layer with remaining cereal and banana slices, and then serve.

Nutritional Information per Serving:

Calories: 196 Cal; Total Fat: 3 g; Saturated Fat: 1 g; Cholesterol: 4 mg; Carbohydrates: 42 g; Fiber: 4 g; Sugar 19 g; Protein: 6 g;

Whole-Wheat Waffles

Yield: 8 waffles, 1 waffle per serving

Preparation Time: 10 minutes

Cooking Time: 20 minutes

Total Time: 30 minutes

Difficulty: Level 1

MAIN INGREDIENTS:

- 1 ½ tablespoon whole-wheat flour
- 1 teaspoon vanilla extract, unsweetened
- 1/3 cup butter, unsalted
- 2 tablespoons maple syrup
- 1 ½ cup whole milk
- 1 egg, at room temperature

Extra Ingredients:

- 2 teaspoons baking powder
- ¼ teaspoon salt

DIRECTIONS:

Adult:
 Switch on the waffle iron and then let it preheat.
Kid:
 Place butter in a medium heatproof bowl and then microwave it for 1 minute or more until it is melted completely.
 Add eggs into the melted butter, add vanilla and maple syrup and then whisk until combined.
 Take a separate medium bowl, add flour in it, add salt and baking powder and then stir until combined.
 Add ½ cup of the flour mixture into the egg mixture, whisk until smooth, and then continue whisking remaining flour, ½ cup at a time, until smooth batter comes together; there shouldn't be any lumps in the batter.
Adult + Kid:
 Ladle ½ cup of the batter into the heated waffle iron, shut with its lid, and then cook for 5 to 7 minutes until rm and golden brown.
 When done, use a tong to transfer cooked waffles to a plate and repeat with the remaining batter.
Kid:
 Drizzle honey over waffles, and serve them with favorite sliced fruits.

Nutritional Information per Serving:

 Calories: 305 Cal; Total Fat: 13 g; Saturated Fat: 4 g; Cholesterol: 170 mg; Carbohydrates: 37 g; Fiber: 5 g; Sugar: 7 g; Protein: 11 g;

Chocolate and Avocado Smoothie

Yield: : 4 glasses, 1 glass per serving

Preparation Time: 5 minutes

Cooking Time: 0 minutes

Total Time: 5 minutes

Difficulty: Level 1

MAIN INGREDIENTS:

- •2 frozen bananas
- •1 medium avocado
- •2 tablespoons flax seeds
- •6 tablespoons cocoa powder
- •2 tablespoons honey
- •2 cups whole milk

DIRECTIONS:

Kid:
Peel the bananas, slice them, and then place them into a food processor.
Cut the avocado in half, remove its pit and then transfer its flesh into a food processor.
Add remaining ingredients, cover with the lid, and then pulse for 30 seconds until smooth.
Divide the smoothie evenly among four glasses and then serve.

Nutritional Information per Serving:

Calories: 339.3 Cal; Total Fat: 3.3 g; Saturated Fat: 1.3 g; Cholesterol: 7.4 mg; Carbohydrates: 44.3 g; Fiber: 6.1 g; Sugar: 13.3 g; Protein: 17.2 g;

Flaxseed and Blueberry Oatmeal

Yield: 2

Preparation Time: 5 minutes

Cooking Time: 10 minutes

Total Time: 15 minutes

Difficulty: Level 1

MAIN INGREDIENTS:

- 1 cup rolled oats, old-fashioned
- 1/3 cup blueberries, fresh
- 2 tablespoons ground flaxseed
- 2 tablespoons chopped pecans, toasted
- 1 cup whole milk ¾ cup of water

Extra Ingredients:

- 1/16 teaspoon salt
- 1 tablespoon honey

DIRECTIONS:

Pour the milk and water in a small saucepan, place it over medium heat, and then bring it to a boil.

Then immediately switch the heat to medium-low level, add flax seeds, oats and salt into the milk and stir ntil mixed.

Cook the oatmeal for 7 minutes until oats turn tender, stirring frequently, and then remove the pan from eat.

Cover the pan with its lid, let the oats rest for 2 minutes, stir it well and then divide evenly between two owls.

Top each bowl of oatmeal with 1 tablespoon pecans and 3 tablespoons berries, drizzle with ½ tablespoon oney and then serve.

Nutritional Information per Serving:

Calories: 340 Cal; Total Fat: 9.4 g; Saturated Fat: 2.6 g; Cholesterol: 2.5 mg; Carbohydrates: 49.2 g; Fiber: 8.3 g; Sugar: 17.7 g; Protein: 11.9 g;

Flaxseed and Raisin Bread

Yield: : 1 bread (16 slices), 2 slices per

Preparation Time: 10 minutes

Cooking Time: 1 hour and 15 minutes

Total Time: 1 hour and 25 minutes

Difficulty: Level 1

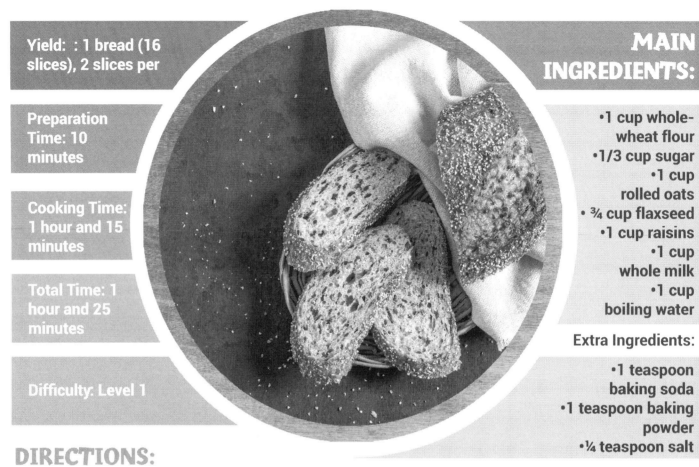

MAIN INGREDIENTS:

- 1 cup whole-wheat flour
- 1/3 cup sugar
- 1 cup rolled oats
- ¾ cup flaxseed
- 1 cup raisins
- 1 cup whole milk
- 1 cup boiling water

Extra Ingredients:

- 1 teaspoon baking soda
- 1 teaspoon baking powder
- ¼ teaspoon salt

DIRECTIONS:

Adult:

Switch on the oven, then set it to 350 degrees F, and let it preheat.

Kid:

Meanwhile, take a 9-by-5 inch loaf pan and grease it with oil.

Take a large bowl, place raisins in it, pour in boiling water, stir in baking soda, and then let the raisins stand for 5 minutes.

Adult + Kid:

Add oats, whole-wheat flour, salt, sugar, and baking powder, stir until just mixed, and then spoon the mixtur into the prepared loaf pan.

Place the loaf pan into the oven and then bake the bread for 1 hour and 15 minutes until the top turns very brown.

When done, let the bread cool for 10 minutes into the pan, lift it out, and then cool the bread completely on wire rack.

Cut the cool bread into sixteen slices and then serve.

Nutritional Information per Serving:

Calories: 260 Cal; Total Fat: 6 g; Saturated Fat: 2 g; Cholesterol: 2 mg; Carbohydrates: 46 g; Fiber: 8 g; Sugar: 7 g; Protein: 4 g;

Chapter 4: Lunch
List of Kid-Friendly Foods for Lunch

Rice – Rice is a staple food in most homes. It is a good source of energy and fiber that keeps you full for a long day.

Chicken (pieces/ minced) – Chicken helps young kids grow taller and stronger. It is a good source of first-class proteins and is filled with different types of amino acids.

Potatoes – Carbohydrates provide a lot of energy, and potatoes are filled with them. They have vitamins B and C, among other nutrients as well. They also help you feel full, and you get hungry less often.

Sweet potatoes – If you are having stomach problems, you could eat sweet potatoes as they are a rich source of fiber. They will keep your bowels healthy.

Bell peppers – They are high in Vitamin A and C, which help in the development of good eyesight and skin. They also help in fighting germs, so you get sick less often.

Soybean – If you don't like eating meat, soybean can be a great alternative. They have hefty amounts of protein and iron. Whole soybeans are best for children as they have all the essential amino acids.

Quinoa – Quinoa might have a funny name, but it has twice as much fiber as any other grain. It will keep your stomach working fine.

Tuna – Tuna is one of the most nutritious fishes to eat. They are high in «good» Omega-3 fatty acids and low in «bad» saturated fats. This is important for healthy growth and development.

Mushrooms – Many people don't know, but you can get calcium without dairy. Eating mushrooms is one way to built-up calcium if you don't like milk. They are also rich sources of iron that prevent anemia in children.

Whole-wheat pasta – Regular pasta has a lot of nutrients taken away from it. Eating whole wheat pasta increases fiber intake and helps you feel fuller for longer.

Tuna Salad Sandwich

Yield: 2 sandwiches, I sandwich per serving

Preparation Time: 10 minutes

Cooking Time: 0 minutes

Total Time: 10 minutes

Difficulty: Level 1

MAIN INGREDIENTS:

- 6 ounces of canned tuna
- 2 leaves of lettuce
- 1 ½ tablespoon sweet pickle relish
- 2 ½ tablespoons mayonnaise
- 2 slices of American cheese
- 4 slices of whole-wheat bread

DIRECTIONS:

Kid:

Drain the tuna, and then place it in a bowl.

Add pickle relish and mayonnaise and then stir until mixed.

Toast the bread slices in the toaster until golden brown on both sides.

Prepare the sandwich and for this, layer a toasted bread slice with a lettuce leaf, and then layer with half of the tuna salad.

Top the tuna salad with a cheese slice and then cover the top with another toasted bread slice.

Assemble another sandwich in the same manner and then serve.

Nutritional Information per Serving:

Calories: 189.5 Cal; Total Fat: 9.1 g; Saturated Fat: 1.8 g; Cholesterol: 36.1 mg; Carbohydrates: 6.1 g; Fiber: 0.1 g; Sugar: 2.1 g; Protein: 20 g;

Pepperoni Pizza

Yield: 1 pizza, 1 pizza per serving

Preparation Time: 5 minutes

Cooking Time: 8 minutes

Total Time: 13 minutes

Difficulty: Level 1

MAIN INGREDIENTS:

- •8 slices of pepperoni
- •½ teaspoon dried oregano
- •1 teaspoon olive oil
- • 2 tablespoons shredded mozzarella cheese
- •3 tablespoons pizza sauce
- •2 eggs, at room temperature

DIRECTIONS:

Crack the eggs in a medium bowl, add oregano, and then whisk until combined.

Take a medium skillet pan, place it over medium heat, add oil, and let it heat for 2 minutes.

Pour the egg batter into the skillet pan, rotate the pan to spread it evenly, and then cook it for 3 minutes until the bottom is firm.

Then arrange pepperoni slices on top of the omelet, sprinkle with cheese, cover the pan with its lid, and cook for 2 minutes until the cheese has melted and eggs have set.

When done, slide pizza onto a plate, and then serve it with pizza sauce.

Nutritional Information per Serving:

Calories: 285 Cal; Total Fat: 18 g; Saturated Fat: 6.5 g; Cholesterol: 0 mg; Carbohydrates: 8 g; Fiber: 1 g; Sugar: 2 g; Protein: 22 g;

Funny Face Sandwich

Yield: 2 sandwiches, 1 sandwich per serving

Preparation Time: 10 minutes

Cooking Time: 10 minutes

Total Time: 20 minutes

Difficulty: Level 1

MAIN INGREDIENTS:

- 2 slices of whole-wheat bread
- 2 large strawberries, fresh
- 6 blueberries
- 2 tablespoons peanut butter

DIRECTIONS:

Kid:
 Toast the bread slices in a toaster, and then place them on a cutting board.
 Spread 1 tablespoon of peanut butter on top of each bread slices.
Adult + Kid:
 Cut each strawberry into three round slices.
 If strawberries are not present, you can use a banana to cut out three slices.
Adult + Kid:
 Use two round slices of strawberry to create ears, and place them on each of the top corners on one bread slice, and then place the third slice of strawberry in the space between the ears; this will be the nose.
 Place a blueberry on the strawberry slice for the nose, and then arrange two more blueberries for the eyes.

Nutritional Information per Serving:

 Calories: 243 Cal; Total Fat: 9.7 g; Saturated Fat: 9.5 g; Cholesterol: 27 mg; Carbohydrates: 28.5 g; Fiber: 4.5 g; Sugar: 5.3 g; Protein: 10.3 g;

Sandwich on Skewers

Yield: 2 skewers, 1 skewer per serving

Preparation Time: 10 minutes

Cooking Time: 8 minutes

Total Time: 10 minutes

Difficulty: Level 1

MAIN INGREDIENTS:

•4 slices of whole-wheat bread
•4 slices of bacon
•4 slices of cheese

DIRECTIONS:

Use a cookie cutter of any shape, and then cut out eight bread shapes from the bread slices.
Similarly, cut out cheese and bacon shape from cheese and bacon slices.
Take a skewer and thread four bread shapes, bacon shapes, and cheese shapes in an alternate position.
Assemble another skewer in the same manner and then serve.

Nutritional Information per Serving:

Calories: 614.5 Cal; Total Fat: 30.7 g; Saturated Fat: 14.4 g; Cholesterol: 59 mg; Carbohydrates: 49.2 g; Fiber: 6.6 g; Sugar: 4.9 g; Protein: 35.3 g;

Chicken Parmesan Sliders

Yield: 8 sliders, 2 sliders per serving

Preparation Time: 10 minutes

Cooking Time: 20 minutes

Total Time: 30 minutes

Difficulty: Level 1

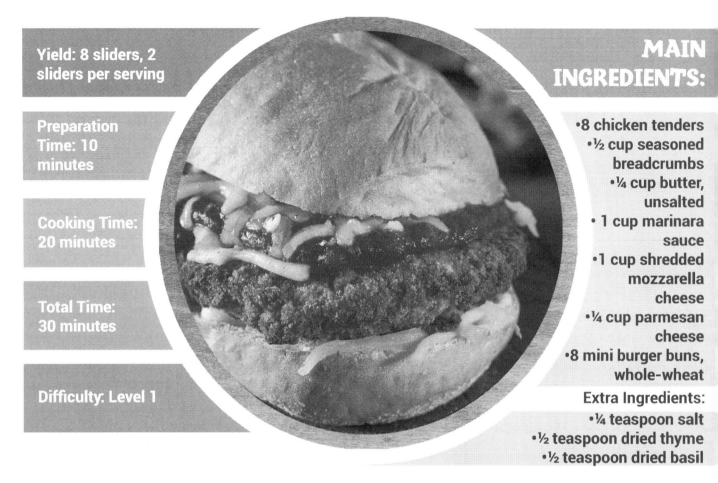

MAIN INGREDIENTS:

- 8 chicken tenders
- ½ cup seasoned breadcrumbs
- ¼ cup butter, unsalted
- 1 cup marinara sauce
- 1 cup shredded mozzarella cheese
- ¼ cup parmesan cheese
- 8 mini burger buns, whole-wheat

Extra Ingredients:
- ¼ teaspoon salt
- ½ teaspoon dried thyme
- ½ teaspoon dried basil

DIRECTIONS:

Switch on the oven, then set it to 400 degrees F, and let it preheat.

Take a baking sheet, grease it with oil, and then set aside until required.

Meanwhile, place bread crumbs in a shallow dish, add salt, thyme, basil, and parmesan cheese, and then stir until combined.

Place butter in a medium bowl and then microwave it for 1 minute or more until it melts.

Stir the melted butter, then take a piece of chicken tender, dip it into the butter and then roll it into the breadcrumbs mixture until coated.

Place the prepared chicken tender on the prepared baking sheet and then repeat with the other chicken tenders.

Place the baking sheet into the oven and then bake the chicken tenders for 15 minutes.

When you finish, remove the baking sheet from the oven and then switch on the broiler.

Cut each burger bun lengthwise, and place the bottom halves on a baking sheet lined with foil.

Place a baked chicken tender into each burger bun, top each chicken tender with 2 tablespoons of marinara sauce and mozzarella cheese, and then cover with the top halves of the burger buns.

Place the baking dish under the broiler, and broil the sandwiches until the cheese melts and turns golden brown.

Serve immediately.

Nutritional Information per Serving:

Calories: 500 Cal; Total Fat: 20 g; Saturated Fat: 10 g; Cholesterol: 90 mg; Carbohydrates: 35 g; Fiber: 16 g; Sugar: 8 g; Protein: 45 g;

Quinoa Fritters

Yield: 6 plates, 1 plate per serving

Preparation Time: 10 minutes

Cooking Time: 20 minutes

Total Time: 30 minutes

Difficulty: Level 1

MAIN INGREDIENTS:

- 2 cups quinoa, cooked
- 1/3 cup white whole-wheat flour
- ½ cup chopped white onion
- 1 tablespoon chopped parsley
- 4 tablespoons olive oil
- 1/3 cup shredded cheddar cheese
- 3 eggs at room temperature

Extra Ingredients:
- ½ teaspoon of sea salt
- ½ teaspoon ground black pepper

DIRECTIONS:

Adult:
   Cook the quinoa according to the instruction on its package and, when done, fluff it with a fork, and then let it cool for 15 minutes.
Kid:
   Transfer quinoa to a large bowl, add onion, parsley, salt, black pepper, and cheese and then stir until combined.
   Crack the eggs in a bowl, whisk until blended, then add to the quinoa mixture and stir until mixed.
   Prepare the fritters and for this, use a tablespoon or a small ice cream scoop to take out some of the quinoa mixture, roll it into a ball, and then place the fritter on a plate.
Adult:
   When ready to cook, place a large skillet pan over medium heat, add oil and let it heat for 3 minutes.
Adult + Kid:
   Then place fritters in the pan and then cook them for 3 to 5 minutes per side, until golden brown on both sides.
   Prepare a plate by lining it with paper towels, place fried fritters on it, and let them rest for 5 minutes.
   Serve the fritters with ketchup.

Nutritional Information per Serving:

Calories: 193 Cal; Total Fat: 6 g; Saturated Fat: 2 g; Cholesterol: 104 mg; Carbohydrates: 26 g; Fiber: 3 g; Sugar: 1 g; Protein: 7 g;

Quinoa Stuffed Mushrooms

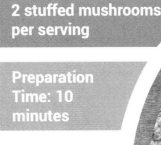

Yield: 8 stuffed mushrooms, 2 stuffed mushrooms per serving

Preparation Time: 10 minutes

Cooking Time: 30 minutes

Total Time: 40 minutes

Difficulty: Level 1

MAIN INGREDIENTS:

- 1 cup uncooked quinoa
- ½ of a medium white onion, peeled, chopped
- 1 chopped celery
- 1 medium red bell pepper, cored, chopped
- 2 cups baby spinach leaves
- 1 large tomato, chopped
- 8 caps of Portabella mushrooms

Extra Ingredients:
- 1 teaspoon olive oil
- 1 cup shredded mozzarella cheese
- 1 ½ cup water

DIRECTIONS:

Adult:
 Switch on the oven, then set it to 400 degrees F and let it preheat.
Adult + Kid:
 Prepare the ingredients and for this, peel the onion, and chop it.
 Remove the stem and seeds of the bell pepper, and then chop it.
 Chop the tomato, and then remove the stem of the mushrooms.
Adult:
 Place oil in a large saucepan, place it over medium-low heat and then heat it for 2 minutes.
Adult + Kid:
 Then add celery, bell pepper, and onion, stir until the vegetables are coated in oil, and then cook for 4 minutes until tender.
 Add tomato and spinach, stir until mixed, and then cook for 2 minutes until spinach leaves wilt.
 Add quinoa, pour in the water, stir, switch heat to a high level, and then bring the mixture to a boil.
 Then, reduce heat to the low level, cover the pan with its lid, and then simmer for 10 minutes until the quinoa turnstender.
 Add cheese, stir until combined, and then remove the pan from heat.
Kid:
 Take a 13-by-9 inch rimmed baking sheet, place mushrooms in it. and then fill them with the quinoa mixture.
Adult:
 Place prepared mushrooms into the oven, and bake them for 10 minutes. until the mushrooms are thoroughly heated, and the cheese has melted.
 Serve immediately.

Nutritional Information per Serving:

Calories: 394 Cal; Total Fat: 15 g; Saturated Fat: 5 g; Cholesterol: 36 mg; Carbohydrates: 42 g; Fiber: 7 g; Sugar: 14 g; Protein: 25 g;

Avocado and Cheese Toasties

Yield: 4 toasties, 2 toasties per serving

Preparation Time: 10 minutes

Cooking Time: 10 minutes

Total Time: 20 minutes

Difficulty: Level 1

MAIN INGREDIENTS:

- ½ of a medium avocado
- 4 slices of cheddar cheese
- 2 tablespoons butter, unsalted
- 4 slices of whole-wheat bread

DIRECTIONS:

Kid:

Scoop the flesh of the avocado into a medium and then mash it by using a fork.

Take two bread slices, and then spread ½ tablespoon of butter on one side of each bread slice.

Switch on the sandwich press, place a buttered bread slice in it butter-side down, and then spread half of he mashed avocado on top.

Cover the avocado layer with two cheese slices, top with another buttered bread slice butter-side-up, and hen close the sandwich press.

Let the sandwich cook until it's golden brown on all sides, and when done, transfer it to a plate.

Prepare another sandwich in the same manner and then serve.

Nutritional Information per Serving:

Calories: 385.8 Cal; Total Fat: 14.4 g; Saturated Fat: 2.1 g; Cholesterol: 8.6 mg; Carbohydrates: 54.5 g; Fiber: 7.9 g; Sugar: 2.1 g; Protein: 12.6 g;

Mashed Potato Pancakes

Yield: 12 cakes, 4 cakes per serving

Preparation Time: 10 minutes

Cooking Time: 15 minutes

Total Time: 25 minutes

Difficulty: Level 2

MAIN INGREDIENTS:

- 4 medium potatoes
- ¼ cup grated parmesan cheese
- 1 egg, at room temperature
- 7 tablespoons white whole-wheat flour
- 2 tablespoons olive oil

DIRECTIONS:

Take a medium pot, place potatoes in it, and then pour in water; water should be 1-inch over the top of the potatoes.

Adult:

Place the pot over medium-high heat, bring to a boil, and then continue boiling the potatoes for 15 minutes

Adult + Kid:

Check the potatoes by inserting a fork in them, and if it goes in and out easily, then the potatoes are boiled

Kid:

Then rinse the potatoes under cold water, peel them, and cut them into slices.

Place potato slices in a large bowl, mash them with a fork, add egg, cheese, and 3 tablespoons flour, and then stir until combined.

Take a shallow dish, and place the remaining flour in it.

Use an ice cream scoop to take out some of the potato mixtures, shape it into a patty, and then coat it in the flour.

Place the potato cake on a plate, and then repeat with the remaining potato mixture.

Adult:

Place a large skillet pan over medium heat, add oil, and then let it heat for 3 minutes.

Adult + Kid:

Then, arrange the potato cakes into the pan, and then cook them for 3 minutes per side until golden brown

Serve straight away.

Nutritional Information per Serving:

Calories: 226 Cal; Total Fat: 15 g; Saturated Fat: 7 g; Cholesterol: 15 mg; Carbohydrates: 19 g; Fiber: 6 g; Sugar: 3 g; Protein: 3 g;

Sweet Potato Wedges

Yield: 4 plates, 1 plate per serving

Preparation Time: 10 minutes

Cooking Time: 35 minutes

Total Time: 45 minutes

Difficulty: Level 1

MAIN INGREDIENTS:

- 4 medium sweet potatoes
- 2 teaspoons paprika
- 2 tablespoons olive oil

DIRECTIONS:

Adult:
Switch on the oven, then set it to 400 degrees F, and let it preheat.
Kid:
Scrub the potatoes, cut off their ends, and then wash them.
Working on one potato at a time, cut it into eight wedges lengthwise, and then place the wedges in a large bowl.
Drizzle oil over the wedges, sprinkle with paprika, and then toss until all the wedges are coated in oil and paprika.
Adult + Kid:
Take a rimmed baking sheet, spread the potato wedges in a single layer, and then bake them for 30 to 35 minutes until cooked and golden brown, turning halfway.
Kid:
When done, let the wedges cool for 5 minutes, and then serve with a favorite dip.

Nutritional Information per Serving:

Calories: 88 Cal; Total Fat: 3 g; Saturated Fat: 1 g; Cholesterol: 20 mg; Carbohydrates: 13 g; Fiber: 2 g; Sugar: g; Protein: 1 g;

Popcorn Chicken

Yield: 4

Preparation Time: 10 minutes

Cooking Time: 25 minutes

Total Time: 35 minutes

Difficulty: Level 2

MAIN INGREDIENTS:

- 1 pound chicken breast, skinless
- ½ teaspoon ground black pepper
- ¼ teaspoon cayenne pepper
- 1 cup bread crumbs
- ¼ cup cornmeal
- 1 egg, at room temperature
- ¼ cup grated parmesan cheese

Extra Ingredients:

- 1 teaspoon salt

DIRECTIONS:

Adult:

Switch on the oven, then set it to 400 degrees F, and let it preheat.

Kid:

Take a rimmed baking sheet. and then grease it with oil.

Cut the chicken into 1-inch pieces, place them in a large bowl, add salt and black pepper and then toss until coated.

Crack the egg in a medium bowl, and then whisk until beaten.

Take a shallow dish, place bread crumbs in it, add cornmeal, salt, cayenne pepper, and cheese and then stir until mixed.

Take a piece of a chicken, dip it into the egg by using a fork, coat it in bread crumbs mixture, and then place it on a baking sheet.

Adult + Kid:

Repeat with the remaining chicken pieces, place them on a baking sheet, and then bake for 25 minutes until golden brown, flipping the chicken pieces halfway.

Serve chicken popcorns with a favorite dip.

Nutritional Information per Serving:

Calories: 351 Cal; Total Fat: 22 g; Saturated Fat: 4 g; Cholesterol: 40 mg; Carbohydrates: 21 g; Fiber: 1 g; Sugar: 0 g; Protein: 18 g;

Ranch Chicken Tenders

Yield: 2 plates

Preparation Time: 10 minutes

Cooking Time: 30 minutes

Total Time: 40 minutes

Difficulty: Level 1

MAIN INGREDIENTS:

- 1 pound chicken breast, skinless
- 2 cups white whole-wheat flour
- 1 bag of ranch Doritos, regular size
- ¼ teaspoon salt
- ¼ teaspoon ground black pepper
- 2 eggs, at room temperature

DIRECTIONS:

Adult:
Switch on the oven, then 350 degrees F, and let it preheat.
Kid:
Take a baking sheet, line it with parchment sheet, and then set aside until it is required.
Meanwhile, place the Doritos in a food processor, and then pulse until the mixture resembles fine crumbs.
You can also smash the bag with a rolling pin, and then transfer it into a shallow bowl.
Crack eggs in another shallow bowl, and then beat them with a fork until combined.
Place flour in another shallow dish, add salt and black pepper, and then stir until combined.
Cut the chicken into strips, and then, working on one chicken strip at a time, coat it with flour, dip into eggs, coat with Dorito, and then place it on a baking sheet.
Repeat with the remaining chicken strips, and place them on the baking sheet with some distance.
Adult + Kid:
Bake the chicken strips for 30 minutes until they are tender and golden brown, turning halfway, and then serve.

Nutritional Information per Serving:

Calories: 112 Cal; Total Fat: 6.2 g; Saturated Fat: .1 g; Cholesterol: 17 mg; Carbohydrates: 7.1 g; Fiber: 0.3 g; Sugar: 0.1 g; Protein: 7 g;

Baked Chicken Meatballs

Yield: 16 meatballs, 4 meatballs per serving

Preparation Time: 10 minutes

Cooking Time: 26 minutes

Total Time: 36 minutes

Difficulty: Level 1

MAIN INGREDIENTS:

- 1 pound ground chicken
- ¾ cup Italian breadcrumbs
- 1 egg, at room temperature
- ½ cup shredded parmesan cheese

DIRECTIONS:

Adult:

Switch on the oven, then set it to 400 degrees F, and let it preheat.

Kid:

Take a rimmed baking sheet, line it with foil, and then spray it with oil.

Take a large bowl, place all the ingredients in it, and then stir until it is well combined.

Divide the chicken mixture into sixteen portions, with each portion as about 2 tablespoons, and then roll each portion into a ball.

Adult + Kid:

Arrange the meatballs on a baking sheet, bake them for 24 to 26 minutes until golden brown and thoroughly cooked.

Serve straight away.

Nutritional Information per Serving:

Calories: 200 Cal; Total Fat: 9.4 g; Saturated Fat: 3.3 g; Cholesterol: 100 mg; Carbohydrates: 10 g; Fiber: 0.6 g; Sugar: 0.9 g; Protein: 18.4 g;

Cheesy Chicken Tacos

Yield: 12 tacos, 2 tacos per serving

Preparation Time: 10 minutes

Cooking Time: 22 minutes

Total Time: 32 minutes

Difficulty: Level 1

MAIN INGREDIENTS:

- 16 ounces refried beans
- 2 cups cooked shredded chicken
- 1 medium white onion, peeled, chopped
- 4.5 ounces green chilies
- 1 cup of salsa
- 1 ½ cups shredded Pepper Jack cheese
- 12 taco shells

Extra Ingredients:

- 1 teaspoon salt
- ½ teaspoon ground black pepper
- 1 tablespoon ground cumin
- 1 tablespoon olive oil

DIRECTIONS:

Adult:
Switch on the oven, then set it to 375 degrees F, and let it preheat.
Place a large skillet pan over medium heat, add oil, and let it heat for 2 minutes.
Adult + Kid:
Add onion, stir until coated, and then cook it for 6 minutes until tender.
Add salt, black pepper, and cumin, stir until combined, and then add chicken, green chilies, and salsa.
Stir until mixed, cook the chicken for 3 to 5 minutes until hot, and then remove the pan from heat.
Take a baking dish, and spread some beans in the form of a thin layer in it.
Divide the beans in remaining taco shells, top with the chicken mixture and cheese, and then bake for 10 minutes, until the cheese melts.
Serve straight away.

Nutritional Information per Serving:

Calories: 486 Cal; Total Fat: 14 g; Saturated Fat: 5 g; Cholesterol: 34.6 mg; Carbohydrates: 75.6 g; Fiber: 10 g; Sugar: 2 g; Protein: 17.8 g;

Cheesy Rice

Yield: 4 plates, 1 plate per serving

Preparation Time: 5 minutes

Cooking Time: 12 minutes

Total Time: 17 minutes

Difficulty: Level 1

MAIN INGREDIENTS:

- 1 ½ cup brown rice
- 2 cups chopped broccoli florets
- ½ teaspoon garlic powder
- ¼ teaspoon salt
- 2 tablespoons of butter, unsalted
- 1 cup shredded cheddar cheese
- 4 cups of water

DIRECTIONS:

Adult + Kid:
 Pour water in a large pot, place it over medium heat. and then bring it to a simmer.
 Add rice, cook for 10 minutes or until tender, then drain the rice, and let it sit for 5 minutes.
 Take a heatproof bowl, place chopped broccoli florets, cover the bowl with a plastic wrap, and then microwave for 2 minutes or more until steamed and tender.
 Kid:
 Return rice into the pot, drain the broccoli, and then add it into the rice.
 Add garlic, salt, butter, and cheese, stir until mixed, and then serve.

Nutritional Information per Serving:

 Calories: 439 Cal; Total Fat: 17.2 g; Saturated Fat: 9.3 g; Cholesterol: 43.2 mg; Carbohydrates: 58.4 g; Fiber: 3.6 g; Sugar: 0.9 g; Protein: 13.2 g;

Chapter5: Dinner List of Kid-Friendly Foods for Dinner

Halibut – It is one of the good choices of fish that you can eat for a healthy dinner. The fish is rich in Omega-3s, which is important for a growing child. It has lots of vitamins as well.

Cod – Cod is also a flavorful fish that can be the star of a hearty meal. It is nutritious and is filled with Vitamin D, which helps the development of bones. It is also an excellent choice for children having type I diabetes.

Salmon – One of the tastiest fish on this list is salmon. They are packed with Omega-3s, especially in DHA, which is vital for young mind development. They make a great part of the brain cell.

Shrimps – You should eat not only fish but also try different types of seafood. Shrimps are considered a delicacy, and they have harder to find nutrients filled in them. They have choline, copper, selenium, and iodine. They also have cancer-fighting antioxidants.

Beef (cuts/minced) – Beef is considered as an essential part of a child's diet because it contains almost all the nutrition a child needs for good growth. It is a source of high-quality protein, iron, and zinc. It also has vitamins B6 and B12.

Broccoli – Do not be too picky about food. All vegetables provide unique benefits, and you need to accept all of them. If you get the flu often, then try introducing broccoli in your dinner meals. They boost the immune system and also prevent ulcers from developing.

Carrot – Everybody knows that they are great for your eyes. They have high Vitamins A, but they also are good for healthy teeth and gums. They are crunchy and add texture to your dinner plate.

Cauliflower – Cauliflower is a beautiful vegetable that can be made in a variety of ways. Different styles of dinner can be served to showcase cauliflower. It is good for your skin as it contains sulforaphane. It protects your skin from harmful UV light and excessive sunlight.

Cabbage – Cabbages are seen everywhere in salads and fillings for burgers, but they can make a great dinner by themselves as well. They have a great fiber content that saves your digestive tract from a lot of problems.

Kale – Leafy greens are one of the most nutritious food groups to eat. Kale is also a good source of plant-based calcium, and they have no fat or sugar content. It is not always accepted by children, so you must introduce them to children's diets at a young age.

Pumpkin – Pumpkins are sweet and very flavourful and can be easily added to many kinds of dishes. They are low in fat and are filled with fiber, antioxidants, and different types of minerals and vitamins.

Butternut squash – This squash is extremely beneficial for children as it reduces the chances of infections. It also reduces inflammation. It is filled with fiber, antioxidants, vitamins, and minerals.

Sweet potato – Sweet potatoes have an ample supply of Vitamin A and beta-carotene. They also boost immunity so you can fight harmful chemicals and germs.

Tomato – Tomatoes have a high source of Vitamin A and alpha/beta-carotene. It has high levels of cancer preventing antioxidants. Numerous studies have shown that tomatoes reduce the chances of kids getting lead toxicity, which leads to brain impairment. Tomatoes are extremely versatile and can form a base of any broth and gravy for dinner.

Papaya – Children sometimes develop intestinal worms; papaya is a great food to get rid of them. It also improves metabolism, which reduces stomach aches.

Green peas – They can be incorporated in any meal and can also become the center of a main for dinner. They are packed with goodness. Nutrients such as Vitamin C and K are presently providing good skin health. They also are great for bone and brain development.

Lentil – They are a great source of carbohydrates and energy. Preparing one or two cups of it provides a lot of benefits for everyone. They are high in folate, which is important for the nervous system. It also boosts immunity and helps the body fight germs.

Legume – Legumes are one of the foods that boost height in children. They are also rich in many essential vitamins and minerals, such as Vitamin B types, zinc, magnesium, and calcium. Like lentils, they have a lot of folate in them that is necessary for brain development.

Black beans – Beans can be served in a variety of ways and are enjoyed by many people. Children should eat beans more often because they are high in plant-based proteins. They are also rich in fiber that curbs hunger.

Navy beans – They are the fiber kings; a hearty serving of them will make you feel full for an entire day. They have both soluble and insoluble fiber, giving the benefits of both. They help in regulating blood sugar levels too.

Couscous – Couscous is low in fat, and it contains different minerals and vitamins. It has a rich source of selenium. It is are an excellent choice for dinners because it is easy to prepare.

Whole-wheat spaghetti – If you want to eat healthily, always opt for whole wheat instead of refined food products. The same goes for spaghetti. There are hundreds of dishes made by spaghetti that can easily be your dinner. Whole wheat spaghetti has more protein, fiber, and overall nutrients. it is more filling, and you will get hungry less.

Black Bean Burgers

Yield: 3 burgers, 1 burger per serving

Preparation Time: 10 minutes

Cooking Time: 8 minutes

Total Time: 18 minutes

Difficulty: Level 1

MAIN INGREDIENTS:

- .5 ounces canned black beans
- ¼ cup chopped white onion
- 2 2/3 tablespoons bread crumbs
- ¼ cup cornmeal
- 1 small egg, at room temperature
- 2 tablespoons olive oil

Extra Ingredients:

- 3 whole-wheat hamburger buns
- 3 leaves of lettuce
- 3 slices of cheddar cheese

DIRECTIONS:

Kid:
 Peel the onion and chop it, crack the egg in a small bowl, and then whisk it lightly.
 Drain the beans, place them in a medium bowl, and then mash with a fork until broken.
 Add chopped onion, bread crumbs, and onion and then stir until well combined.
Kid + Adult:
 Divide the mixture into three portions and then shape each portion into a patty.
 Place cornmeal in a shallow dish and then dredge each patty until coated.
 Place a medium skillet pan over medium-high heat, add oil, and let it heat until warm.
 Add the prepared patties into the pan and then cook them for 2 to 3 minutes per side until golden brown.
 When done, transfer the patties to a plate lined with paper towelsl and let them rest for 5 minutes.
 Meanwhile, cut each bun in half lengthwise, and then toast them until warm and golden brown.
Kid:
 Assemble the burger and for this, take a bottom half of the burger bun, arrange a lettuce leaf on it, and then top with a fried black bean patty.
 Place a cheese slice on the patty, cover with the top half of the bun, and then prepare the remaining two burgers in the same manner.
 Serve burgers with salsa or ketchup.

Nutritional Information per Serving:

Calories: 300 Cal; Total Fat: 6 g; Saturated Fat: 1 g; Cholesterol: 35 mg; Carbohydrates: 50 g; Fiber: 7 g; Sugar: 5 g; Protein: 13 g;

Tomato Spaghetti

Yield: 16 meatballs, 4 meatballs per serving

Preparation Time: 5 minutes

Cooking Time: 28 minutes

Total Time: 33 minutes

Difficulty: Level 2

MAIN INGREDIENTS:

- ½ bunch of basil, fresh
- 2 cans of whole peeled tomatoes, each about
- 14-ounce
- 1 medium white onion
- 1 teaspoon minced garlic
- 1 tablespoon olive oil
- 1 tablespoon balsamic vinegar
- 1 pound whole-wheat spaghetti, uncooked

Extra Ingredients:

- ½ ounce parmesan cheese
- ¾ teaspoon salt
- ¼ teaspoon ground black pepper

DIRECTIONS:

Pick the basil leaves, chop the stalks and three-fourth of the leaves and then reserve the remaining leaves for garnishing.

Peel the onion and then slice it, and then open the tomato can.

Grate the cheese and set it aside until required.

Adult:

Place a medium saucepan over medium heat, add oil and let it heat until warm.

Add sliced onion, stir until just mixed, and then cook for 7 minutes until golden and softened.

Kid + Adult:

Add basil stalks and garlic, stir until mixed, cook for 1 minute, and add canned tomatoes.

Break the tomatoes with the back of your spoon, stir in vinegar, salt, black pepper and then let the sauce cook for 3 minutes, covering the pan with its lid and stirring the sauce occasionally.

Then add chopped basil leaves, and continue cooking the sauce for 12 minutes. **Adult:**

Meanwhile, place a large pot filled with 16 cups of water over medium-high heat, and bring it to a boil.

Then add spaghetti, cook it for 7 t0 8 minutes, or for the time stated on the package until it is al dente; this means spaghetti should be firm and soft enough to eat.

When spaghetti has cooked, reserve ¼ cup of the pasta liquid, drain the spaghetti into a colander, and set aside until required. **Kid:**

When 12 minutes are over, then switch the heat of tomato sauce to the low level, and then pour in enough pasta liquid until the sauce has turned semi-thick.

Continue cooking the sauce for 2 to 3 minutes or until beginning to bubble, add the cooked spaghetti, and then toss it well by using tongs until well coated.

Sprinkle basil leaves and cheese on top, divide spaghetti evenly among four plates, and then serve.

Nutritional Information per Serving:

Calories: 271 Cal; Total Fat: 4.7 g; Saturated Fat: 0.7 g; Cholesterol: 0 mg; Carbohydrates: 49 g; Fiber: 4.7 g; Sugar: 5.9 g; Protein: 9.4 g;

Vegetable Wraps

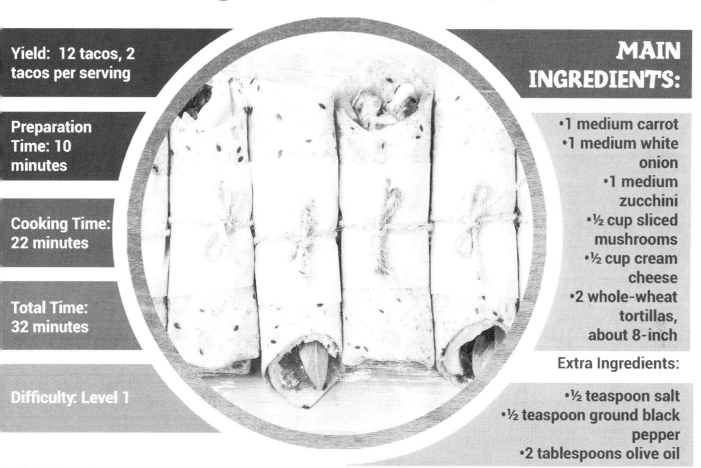

Yield: 12 tacos, 2 tacos per serving

Preparation Time: 10 minutes

Cooking Time: 22 minutes

Total Time: 32 minutes

Difficulty: Level 1

MAIN INGREDIENTS:

- 1 medium carrot
- 1 medium white onion
- 1 medium zucchini
- ½ cup sliced mushrooms
- ½ cup cream cheese
- 2 whole-wheat tortillas, about 8-inch

Extra Ingredients:

- ½ teaspoon salt
- ½ teaspoon ground black pepper
- 2 tablespoons olive oil

DIRECTIONS:

Adult:
Switch on the oven, then set its temperature to 450 degrees F, and let it preheat.
Kid:
Peel the carrot, onion, and zucchini, and then cut the vegetables in ¼-inch thick slices lengthwise.
Transfer the carrot and onion in a medium bowl, add 1 tablespoon oil, ¼ teaspoon salt, and black pepper, and then toss until coated.
Spread the vegetables on a sheet pan, carefully place it into the preheated oven, and then let it bake for 10 minutes.
Meanwhile, place mushroom and zucchini into the bowl, add remaining oil, salt, and black pepper, and then toss until coated.
After 10 minutes of roasting, remove the sheet pan from the oven, add mushrooms and zucchini, then return the sheet pan into the oven, and continue roasting the vegetables for 10 minutes.
When vegetables have roasted, place tortillas on a clean working space, and then spread ¼ cup of cream cheese on top of each tortilla, leaving a 1-inch border.
Use a tong to divide roasted vegetables on the prepared tortillas.
Working on one tortilla at a time, fold it by folding its left and right side over vegetables, and then roll up the tortilla from the tortilla.
Roll up the other tortilla in the same manner, and then cut each wrap in half.
Serve immediately.

Nutritional Information per Serving:

Calories: 498 Cal; Total Fat: 29 g; Saturated Fat: 10 g; Cholesterol: 60 mg; Carbohydrates: 48 g; Fiber: 7 g; Sugar: 7 g; Protein: 10 g;

Sweet Potato and Black Bean Quesadilla

Yield: 2 quesadillas, 1 quesadilla per serving

Preparation Time: 10 minutes

Cooking Time: 20 minutes

Total Time: 30 minutes

Difficulty: Level 1

MAIN INGREDIENTS:

- 1 medium sweet potato
- ½ can black beans, about 14 ounces
- 2 tablespoons cilantro leaves
- ½ tablespoon taco seasoning
- 4 whole-wheat tortillas, about 8-inch
- ½ cup shredded cheddar cheese

DIRECTIONS:

Kid:

Prick the sweet potato using a fork, place it in a microwave, and then cook for 5 minutes at a high heat setting.

After 5 minutes, remove sweet potato from the microwave, cool it for 5 minutes, and then cut the potato half lengthwise.

Scoop the flesh of sweet potato in a medium bowl, and then mash with a fork until smooth.

Add taco seasoning, cilantro, and black beans, and then stir until mixed.

Adult:

Place a large skillet pan over medium heat, and let it heat until hot.

Kid:

Place a tortilla on a clean working space, spread half of the sweet potato mixture on top, sprinkle with ¼ cup of cheese, and then top with the second tortilla.

Adult:

Carefully place prepared quesadilla into the hot pan, cook it for 4 minutes until the cheese melts, then flip the quesadilla, and continue cooking for 2 minutes.

Transfer cooked quesadilla to a plate, prepare another quesadilla using remaining tortillas, sweet potato mixture, and cheese and then cook it.

Serve straight away.

Nutritional Information per Serving:

Calories: 293 Cal; Total Fat: 9 g; Saturated Fat: 3.6 g; Cholesterol: 20 mg; Carbohydrates: 35 g; Fiber: 10 g; Sugar: 2 g; Protein: 17 g;

Vegetable Soup

Yield: 4 bowls, 1 bowl per serving

Preparation Time: 10 minutes

Cooking Time: 40 minutes

Total Time: 50 minutes

Difficulty: Level 2

MAIN INGREDIENTS:

- ½ of a medium head of cauliflower
- 4 medium carrots
- 1 medium white onion, peeled, diced
- 1 large tomato, diced
- 1 ½ cup kale, fresh
- 1 teaspoon minced garlic
- 4 cups vegetable broth

Extra Ingredients:

- 1 teaspoon salt
- ½ teaspoon ground black pepper
- 1 tablespoon olive oil

DIRECTIONS:

Adult:
 Peel the onion and carrot, and then dice the vegetables and tomato.
Kid:
 Tear the leaves of kale, and then tear the cauliflower florets.
Adult:
 Place a large pot over medium heat, add oil, and let it heat until hot.
Adult + Kid:
 Add onion and garlic, stir in 1/8 teaspoon salt, and cook the vegetables for 4 minutes.
 Add carrots, stir in 1/8 teaspoon salt, and then continue cooking for 4 minutes.
 Add cauliflower florets, stir in ½ teaspoon salt and continue cooking for 3 minutes.
Kid:
 Add kale leaves, add 1/8 teaspoon salt, stir until mixed, and then cook the vegetables for 4 minutes.
Adult + Kid:
 Pour in the vegetable broth, stir in remaining salt and black pepper, switch heat to a high level, and boil the soup for 3 minutes, covering the pot with its lid.
 Switch heat to the low level, simmer the soup for 20 minutes, and then stir in tomatoes.
 Continue cooking the soup for 2 minutes, remove the pot from heat, stir the soup and then ladle it evenly among four bowls.
 Serve straight away.

Nutritional Information per Serving:

Calories: 167 Cal; Total Fat: 7 g; Saturated Fat: 1 g; Cholesterol: 0 mg; Carbohydrates: 23 g; Fiber: 6 g; Sugar: 1 g; Protein: 4 g;

Tomato Soup

Yield: 4 bowls, 1 bowl per serving

Preparation Time: 5 minutes

Cooking Time: 50 minutes

Total Time: 55 minutes

Difficulty: Level 1

MAIN INGREDIENTS:

- 1 medium white onion, diced
- 2 cans of diced tomatoes with liquid, each about 1
- 4.5 ounce
- 1 teaspoon minced garlic
- ¼ teaspoon dried thyme
- 2 tablespoons flour
- 1 ½ tablespoon olive oil
- 2 cups vegetable broth

Extra Ingredients:

- ¾ teaspoon sea salt
- ¼ teaspoon ground black pepper

DIRECTIONS:

Adult:
 Place a large pot over medium heat, add oil and let it heat.
Adult + Kid:
 Add onion and garlic into the pot and then cook for 9 minutes until the onion turns soft.
 Stir in the flour, add tomatoes and thyme, pour in the broth, and then stir until combined.
Kid:
 Add salt and black pepper and stir until combined.
Adult + Kid:
 Cover the pot with its lid and then simmer the soup for 40 minutes until cooked.
 Remove the pot from the heat, let it cool for 5 minutes, and then puree it by using an immersion blender for 1 to 2 minutes until smooth yet lumpy.
 If an immersion blender is not available, blend the soup in a food processor, one-fourth of its portion at a time, and then return it into the pot.
 Place the pot over medium heat, and then cook it for 2 minutes until hot.
 Ladle the soup among four bowls and then serve.

Nutritional Information per Serving:

Calories: 130 Cal; Total Fat: 5 g; Saturated Fat: 1 g; Cholesterol: 0 mg; Carbohydrates: 18 g; Fiber: 7 g; Suga 7 g; Protein: 2 g;

Lima Bean Stew

Yield: 5 bowls, 1 bowl per serving

Preparation Time: 5 minutes

Cooking Time: 12 minutes

Total Time: 17 minutes

Difficulty: Level 2

MAIN INGREDIENTS:

- 2 jars of lima beans, each about
- 12 ounces
- 1 medium white onion, peeled, diced
- 2 teaspoons minced garlic
- 2 tablespoons red chili paste
- 1 tablespoon olive oil
- 1 cup of water
- 1 cup tomato sauce

Extra Ingredients:

- 1 teaspoon salt
- ½ teaspoon ground black pepper

DIRECTIONS:

Adult:
  Place a large saucepan over medium heat, add oil and when hot, add onion and garlic and then cook for 5 minutes or until softened.

Adult + Kid:
  Stir in red chili paste, cook for 1 minute, add beans and tomato sauce, and then pour in water.
  Stir until combined, switch heat to the low level, and then cook the stew for 5 minutes or more until hot.
  Season the stew with salt and black pepper, ladle it evenly among five bowls, and then serve.

Nutritional Information per Serving:

Calories: 174 Cal; Total Fat: 3 g; Saturated Fat: 0 g; Cholesterol: 0 mg; Carbohydrates: 31 g; Fiber: 7 g; Sugar: 4 g; Protein: 9 g;

Mushroom Sliders

Yield: 4 sliders, 1 slider per serving

Preparation Time: 35 minutes

Cooking Time: 10 minutes

Total Time: 45 minutes

Difficulty: Level 3

MAIN INGREDIENTS:

• 2 portabella mushrooms
• 8 slices of red onion
• 8 slices of tomato
• 8 small whole-grain dinner rolls
• ¼ cup balsamic vinaigrette

Extra Ingredients:

• ½ teaspoon salt
• 1/3 teaspoon ground black pepper

DIRECTIONS:

Kid:

Remove the stem from each mushroom, then place mushrooms in a plastic bag, and then add the vinaigrette.

Seal the bag, turn it upside down until mushrooms have coated with the vinaigrette, and then let them marinate for 30 minutes at room temperature.

Adult:

Meanwhile, slice the tomato and onion, and set aside until required.

After 30 minutes, remove mushrooms from the plastic bag, drain them, and then season both sides with black pepper and salt.

Adult:

Place a grill pan over medium heat, spray it with oil, and let it heat until hot.

Place the seasoned mushrooms on the grill, gill-side down, and then cook for 4 minutes per side until thoroughly cooked and developed grill marks.

When done, transfer grilled mushrooms to a plate lined with paper towels, and then cut each mushroom into the quarter.

Kid:

Assemble the slider and for this, cut the dinner in half, and then place quarter pieces of one mushroom on the bottom half of a dinner roll.

Top the mushroom with 4 slices of onion and tomato, and then cover with the other half of the roll.

Prepare another slider in the same manner and then serve.

Nutritional Information per Serving:

Calories: 165 Cal; Total Fat: 4 g; Saturated Fat: 1 g; Cholesterol: 0 mg; Carbohydrates: 29 g; Fiber: 5 g; Suga 8 g; Protein: 5 g;

Spaghetti with Basil Pesto

Yield: 7 plates, 1 plate per serving

Preparation Time: 10 minutes

Cooking Time: 10 minutes

Total Time: 20 minutes

Difficulty: Level 1

MAIN INGREDIENTS:

- 1 pound whole-wheat spaghetti, uncooked
- 2 cups basil leaves, fresh
- 4 cloves of garlic, peeled
- ¾ cup and 1 tablespoon oil
- ½ cup grated parmesan cheese
- ¾ cup half-and-half

Extra Ingredients:
- 1 ½ teaspoon salt, divided
  ½ teaspoon ground black pepper

DIRECTIONS:

Kid:
Place basil in a blender, add parmesan cheese, garlic cloves, ½ teaspoon salt, and black pepper.

Adult + Kid:
Cover the blender with its lid, pulse for 20 minutes, and then slowly blend in ¾ cup oil until smooth.
Tip the pesto in a medium bowl and set it aside until required.

Adult:
Place a large pot filled with 16 cups of water over medium-high heat, add remaining oil and salt and bring the water to a boil.
Then add spaghetti, cook it for 6 minutes, or the time stated on the package until al dente; this means spaghetti should be firm and soft enough to eat.
Meanwhile, take a medium skillet pan, place it over medium heat, add pesto sauce and then cook it for 2 minutes until hot.
Whisk in half-and-half until incorporated, and then remove the pan from heat.
When spaghetti has cooked, drain the spaghetti into a colander, and then transfer it to the pan containing pesto sauce.
Toss until spaghetti has coated in the sauce, divide the spaghetti evenly among seven plates and then serve.

Nutritional Information per Serving:

Calories: 414 Cal; Total Fat: 31 g; Saturated Fat: 7 g; Cholesterol: 18 mg; Carbohydrates: 24 g; Fiber: 11 g; Sugar: 8 g; Protein: 9 g;

Fish Tacos

Yield: 4 tacos, 2 tacos per serving

Preparation Time: 10 minutes

Cooking Time: 10 minutes

Total Time: 20 minutes

Difficulty: Level 1

MAIN INGREDIENTS:

- 4 taco shells
- 6 ounces white fish fillet
- ½ of a medium avocado
- ½ teaspoon dried basil
- 1 medium tomato
- 1 tablespoon olive oil
- 1 cup shredded lettuce

Extra Ingredients:

- ¼ teaspoon salt
- ¼ teaspoon ground black pepper
- ½ teaspoon ground cumin
- ½ tablespoon red chili powder

DIRECTIONS:

Kid:

Take a shallow dish, place salt, black pepper, cumin, red chili powder, and basil in it and then stir until combined.

Place fish fillet into the seasoning mix and then toss until coated evenly on all sides.

Adult:

Place a large skillet pan over medium heat, add oil and let it heat.

Adult + Kid:

Place the seasoned fish fillet in it and then cook it for 5 minutes per side until golden brown and cooked.

Kid:

When done, use a tong to transfer fish to a cutting board, let it rest for 2 minutes, and then shred it by usin two forks.

Adult:

Read the baking instructions on the package of taco shells, and then bake them.

Chop the tomato and then chop the avocado.

Kid:

Assemble the taco and for this, evenly divide shredded fish among baked taco shells, add lettuce, avocado and tomato and then serve.

Nutritional Information per Serving:

Calories: 367 Cal; Total Fat: 18 g; Saturated Fat: 4 g; Cholesterol: 51 mg; Carbohydrates: 33 g; Fiber: 6 g; Sugar: 10 g; Protein: 20 g;

Shrimp Fried Rice

Yield: 4 plates, 1 plate per serving

Preparation Time: 15 minutes

Cooking Time: 15 minutes

Total Time: 30 minutes

Difficulty: Level 1

MAIN INGREDIENTS:

- ¾ cup frozen peas and carrots
- 8 ounces small shrimps, peeled, deveined
- 2 green onions, minced
- 4 cups cooked brown rice
- 1 tablespoon soy sauce
- 2 tablespoons olive oil
- 3 eggs, at room temperature

Extra Ingredients:

- ¼ teaspoon salt
- 1/8 teaspoon ground black pepper
- 1 teaspoon sesame oil

DIRECTIONS:

Kid:

   Place shrimps in a medium bowl, add cornstarch, salt, and black pepper, stir until mixed, and then let them marinate at room temperature for 10 minutes.

   Crack eggs in a bowl and then beat them lightly.

   Place peas and carrots in a bowl and then defrost them in the microwave oven.

Adult:

   Meanwhile, cook the rice according to the instruction on its package ,and set aside until required.

   Then place a large skillet pan over high heat, let it heat until hot, and then add 1 tablespoon oil.

Adult + Kid:

   Add marinated shrimps to the pan, spread them in the pan so that the shrimps do not overlap, and then fry them for 30 seconds; do not stir.

   Then flip the shrimps, continue frying them for another 30 seconds and transfer shrimps to a plate.

Adult:

   Switch heat to medium level, add eggs, and then cook them for 3 to 4 minutes until scrambled.

   Transfer eggs to the plate containing shrimps and then wipe clean the pan.

   Return pan over high heat, add remaining oil, and when very hot, add green onions and cook for 15 seconds.   **Adult + Kid:**

   Add cooked rice, stir until combined, and then cook for 2 minutes until hot; do not mix.

   Then stir the rice, drizzle with soy sauce, add carrots and peas, eggs and shrimps, drizzle with sesame oil, and then toss until it is well mixed.

   Cook the rice for 3 minutes until hot, then divide evenly among four plates and then serve.

Nutritional Information per Serving:

Calories: 237.6 Cal; Total Fat: 5.8 g; Saturated Fat: 1.2 g; Cholesterol: 168 mg; Carbohydrates: 35.8 g; Fiber: .3 g; Sugar: 0.4 g; Protein: 17.6 g;

Meatloaf

Yield: 1 meatloaf, about 8 slices, 1 slice per serving

Preparation Time: 10 minutes

Cooking Time: 1 hour

Total Time: 1 hour and 10 minutes

Difficulty: Level 3

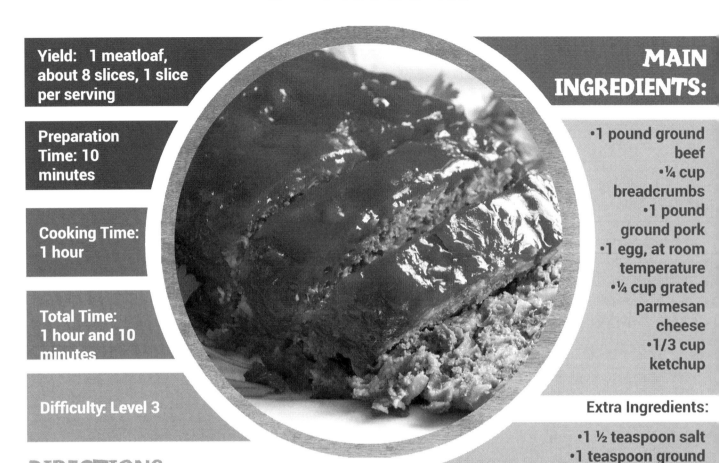

MAIN INGREDIENTS:

- 1 pound ground beef
- ¼ cup breadcrumbs
- 1 pound ground pork
- 1 egg, at room temperature
- ¼ cup grated parmesan cheese
- 1/3 cup ketchup

Extra Ingredients:

- 1 ½ teaspoon salt
- 1 teaspoon ground black pepper

DIRECTIONS:

Adult:
Switch on the oven, then set it to 375 degrees F and let it preheat.

Adult + Kid:
Take a large bowl, place all the ingredients in it, and then stir until well mixed.

Adult:
Take a 9-by-13 inch baking pan, line it with a parchment sheet, and then grease it with oil.

Kid:
Spoon the meat mixture into the pan, press it and spread evenly, and spread some more ketchup on top.

Adult:
Place the baking pan containing meatloaf on the lower rack of the heated oven and then bake for 1 hour until cooked until thoroughly cooked.

When done, use the parchment sheet to take out the meatloaf, let it rest for 15 minutes, and then cut it into eight slices.

Serve straight away.

Nutritional Information per Serving:

Calories: 331 Cal; Total Fat: 18 g; Saturated Fat: 6.4 g; Cholesterol: 123 mg; Carbohydrates: 14 g; Fiber: 1.2 g; Sugar: 6.1 g; Protein: 27 g;

Sloppy Joes

Preparation Time: 10 minutes

Cooking Time: 26 minutes

Total Time: 36 minutes

Difficulty: Level 3

MAIN INGREDIENTS:

- 1 pound ground beef
- ½ of a medium zucchini
- 2 stalks of celery
- ½ of a medium green bell pepper
- 1/3 cup barbecue sauce
- 10 ounces tomato soup
- 4 whole-wheat burger buns

Extra Ingredients:

- 1 teaspoon salt
- ½ teaspoon ground black pepper
- 1 teaspoon paprika
- 1 tablespoon olive oil

DIRECTIONS:

Adult:

Place zucchini in a food processor, add celery and bell pepper, and then puree for 30 seconds or more until smooth.

Take a large skillet pan, place it over medium-high heat, add oil, and let it heat for 2 minutes.

Adult + Kid:

Add blended vegetable mixture into the pan, stir until just mixed, and then cook for 3 to 5 minutes until most of the cooking liquid has evaporated.

Add beef into the pan, break it with the spoon, stir until well mixed with the vegetables and then stir in salt, black pepper, and paprika.

Cook the beef for 8 minutes until thoroughly cooked, add tomato soup and BBQ sauce, and then stir until combined.

Cook the mixture for 10 minutes until thickened, then remove the pan from heat and let the mixture stand for 1 minute.

Cut the bun in half lengthwise, ladle one-fourth of the meat sauce in it, and then serve.

Nutritional Information per Serving:

Calories: 317 Cal; Total Fat: 13.5 g; Saturated Fat: 4.9 g; Cholesterol: 63.5 mg; Carbohydrates: 24 g; Fiber: .5 g; Sugar: 3.5 g; Protein: 23.2 g;

Lentil Soup

Yield: 1

Preparation Time: 10 minutes

Cooking Time: 30 minutes

Total Time: 40 minutes

Difficulty: Level 2

MAIN INGREDIENTS:

- 1 ½ cup lentils, uncooked
- 2 medium white onions
- 1 teaspoon minced garlic
- 4 medium carrots
- 1 cup crushed tomatoes
- 4 cups vegetable stock

Extra Ingredients:

- ½ teaspoon salt
- 1 teaspoon dried thyme
- 2 tablespoons olive oil

DIRECTIONS:

Adult + Kid:

Peel the onions and carrots, dice them, and then transfer into a food processor.

Add garlic, salt, and thyme and then pulse for 30 to 40 seconds until all the vegetables have chopped finely.

Adult:

Place a medium pot over medium heat, add oil, and let it heat for 2 minutes.

Add chopped vegetables, stir until coated in oil, and then cook for 6 minutes or until vegetables begin to soften.

Kid:

Add crushed tomatoes into the pot, pour in the broth, stir until mixed, cover the pot with its lid and then bring it to a boil.

Then, switch heat to medium-low level, add lentil, stir until just mixed, and cover the pot slightly.

Adult:

Simmer the lentils for 20 to 25 minutes until lentils turn soft and to check lentils, take a spoonful of lentil, let it cool slightly, and then taste it, and if it is soft, then lentil has cooked.

Ladle soup evenly among four bowls and then serve.

Nutritional Information per Serving:

Calories: 220.8 Cal; Total Fat: 2 g; Saturated Fat: 0.6 g; Cholesterol: 286 mg; Carbohydrates: 24 g; Fiber: 7.9 g; Sugar: 4 g; Protein: 8 g;

Southwest Couscous

Yield: 4 bowls, 1 bowl per serving

Preparation Time: 10 minutes

Cooking Time: 10 minutes

Total Time: 20 minutes

Difficulty: Level 2

MAIN INGREDIENTS:

- •4 green onions
- •1 packet of whole-wheat couscous, about
- •10-ounces
- •1 can of stewed tomatoes, about
- •14.5 ounces
- •1 can of black beans, about
- •15 ounces
- •1 can of vegetable broth, about
- •14.5 ounces
- •½ cup shredded cheddar cheese
- •2 tablespoons butter, unsalted

Extra Ingredients:

- •1 teaspoon ground cumin
- •1 teaspoon red chili powder

DIRECTIONS:

Adult:
Peel and chop the green onions.
Place a large saucepan over medium heat, add butter and let it melt.
Add three-fourth of the onion, stir until coated in butter, and then cook for 5 to 7 minutes until tender.

Adult + Kid:
Add tomatoes, pour in the broth, stir in chili powder and cumin and then bring it to a boil.
Adult:
Remove pan from heat, add black beans and couscous, stir until mixed, cover the pan with its lid, and then let the couscous stand for 5 minutes.

Adult + Kid:
Fluff the couscous with a fork, divide it evenly among four plates, and then garnish with remaining green onions.
Serve straight away.

Nutritional Information per Serving:

Calories: 316 Cal; Total Fat: 5 g; Saturated Fat: 1 g; Cholesterol: 2 mg; Carbohydrates: 52 g; Fiber: 6 g; Sugar: 3 g; Protein: 14 g;

Chapter 6: Snacks
List of Kid-Friendly Foods for Snacks

Peanut butter – It is extremely delicious, and if you find something good for you that you do not want to eat, try to eat it with peanut butter. It is filled with good fat.

Chickpeas – Chickpea is a rich source of insoluble fiber. This fiber is linked with the prevention of cancer, sugar control, and good digestion. It also has plentiful minerals.

Corn – It has some important nutrients for growth and development. Thiamine, niacin, and folate are essential for good nervous system development.

Cucumber – Cucumber has a lot of Vitamins for the healthy development of kids. It is also very watery and promotes hydration on summer days. It helps reduce stomach problems in children too.

Leafy greens – A healthy diet has green leafy vegetables as its core. They are high in fiber, are a great source of calcium, and have immune-boosting capabilities.

Almonds – Immunity is very important in children's life. Almonds boost up the immune system, so you get sick less often and are not missing school.

Pistachios – Pistachios are a type of nut. They are very low in sugar levels and keep your blood sugar normal. They are also filled with antioxidants and help fight inflammation and cancer.

Hazelnut – These nuts are high in Vitamin E and copper. They have other different types of minerals as well, which makes them very nutritious.

Walnuts – If you want to increase your memory and focus more on your studies, walnuts can help you. They have folate and Omega-3s that boost brain activity.

Sunflower seeds – Seeds and nuts are generally high in fiber. Sunflower seeds also provide fiber. It also has many minerals, such as phosphorus and magnesium.

Flaxseed – It is one of the best plant sources of Omega-3s. They build up good cholesterol in your body, and keeps your heart healthy.

Chickpea Salad

Yield: 4 bowls, 1 bowl per serving

Preparation Time: 10 minutes

Cooking Time: 10 minutes

Total Time: 20 minutes

Difficulty: Level 1

MAIN INGREDIENTS:

- 1 can of chickpeas, about 15 ounces
- 2 medium tomatoes
- 1 dill pickle
- 1 small cucumber
- 1 medium avocado
- ¼ cup chopped scallion
- ½ cup chopped parsley

Extra Ingredients:

- ¼ teaspoon salt
- 1/8 teaspoon ground black pepper
- ½ teaspoon ground cumin
- 2 tablespoons olive oil
- ½ of a lemon

DIRECTIONS:

Kid:

Drain the chickpeas, add them into a bowl, add scallion, avocado, pickle, cucumber, tomato, and parsley and then stir until combined.

Juice the lemon into a small bowl, add salt, black pepper, and cumin and then stir until combined.

Drizzle the lemon juice mixture over the salad and then toss until mixed.

Let the salad chill the refrigerator for 1 hour and then serve.

Nutritional Information per Serving:

Calories: 305 Cal; Total Fat: 18 g; Saturated Fat: 3 g; Cholesterol: 0 mg; Carbohydrates: 29 g; Fiber: 9 g; Sugar: 4 g; Protein: 8 g;

Peanut Butter Hummus

Yield: 44 spoons, 1 spoon per serving

Preparation Time: 5 minutes

Cooking Time: 0 minutes

Total Time: 20 minutes

Difficulty: Level 1

MAIN INGREDIENTS:

- 1 can of chickpeas, about 15 ounces
- 3 tablespoons lemon juice
- ½ teaspoon minced garlic
- ¼ teaspoon salt
- 2 tablespoons olive oil
- 1/3 cup water, warmed
- 4 tablespoons peanut butter

DIRECTIONS:

Kid:
Gather all the ingredients and then place them in a food processor.
Cover the food processor with its lid and then pulse for 30 to 50 seconds until smooth.
Tip the hummus in a bowl and then serve it with vegetable sticks, chips or spread it over bread.

Nutritional Information per Serving:

Calories: 48 Cal; Total Fat: 2 g; Saturated Fat: 0 g; Cholesterol: 0 mg; Carbohydrates: 6 g; Fiber: 1 g; Sugar: 2 g; Protein: 2 g;

Chocolate and Peanut Butter Green Smoothie

Yield: 4 glasses, 1 glass per serving

Preparation Time: 5 minutes

Cooking Time: 0 minutes

Total Time: 20 minutes

Difficulty: Level 1

MAIN INGREDIENTS:

- 1 cup spinach leaves
- 1 ½ frozen banana
- 1 cup baby kale leaves
- 2 tablespoons peanut butter
- 2 cups soy milk, chocolate flavor
- ½ cup of ice cubes

DIRECTIONS:

Kid:
Gather all the ingredients and then place them in a food processor.
Cover the food processor with its lid, and then pulse for 30 to 50 seconds until smooth.
Divide the smoothie among four glasses and then serve.

Nutritional Information per Serving:

Calories: 237 Cal; Total Fat: 10 g; Saturated Fat: 3 g; Cholesterol: 3 mg; Carbohydrates: 36 g; Fiber: 6 g; Sugar: 19 g; Protein: 8 g;

Kale Smoothie

Yield: 2 glasses, 1 glass per serving

Preparation Time: 5 minutes

Cooking Time: 0 minutes

Total Time: 20 minutes

Difficulty: Level 1

MAIN INGREDIENTS:

- •2 frozen bananas
- •2 teaspoons flaxseeds
- •1 cup strawberries, fresh or frozen
- •2 tablespoons peanut butter
- •1 cup kale leaves
- •2 cups whole milk

DIRECTIONS:

Kid:
Gather all the ingredients and then place them in a food processor.
Cover the food processor with its lid and then pulse for 30 to 50 seconds until smooth.
Divide the smoothie among two glasses and then serve.

Nutritional Information per Serving:

Calories: 245 Cal; Total Fat: 5.6 g; Saturated Fat: 0.6 g; Cholesterol: 0 mg; Carbohydrates: 42.3 g; Fiber: 5.7 g; Sugar: 25.8 g; Protein: 9.1 g;

Baked Kale Chips

Yield: 4 plates, 1 plate per serving

Preparation Time: 5 minutes

Cooking Time: 10 minutes

Total Time: 15 minutes

Difficulty: Level 1

MAIN INGREDIENTS:

- 1 bunch of kale
- ¼ teaspoon of sea salt
- ¼ teaspoon smoked paprika
- ¼ teaspoon curry powder
- ¼ teaspoon nutritional yeast
- 1 tablespoon olive oil

DIRECTIONS:

Adult:
 Switch on the oven, then set it to 300 degrees F, and let it preheat.
Kid:
 Meanwhile, tear the kale leaves into pieces, rinse and dry them in a salad spinner.
 Transfer kale leaves into a bowl, drizzle with oil, add salt, paprika, curry powder, and yeast, toss until coated, and massage leaves for 1 to 2 minutes.
 Adult + Kid:
 Take a large baking sheet, line it with parchment sheet, spread kale leaves on it, and then bake them for 10 minutes until kale chips turn dry and crisp.
 When it is done, let the kale chips rest for 5 minutes and then serve them.

Nutritional Information per Serving:

 Calories: 46 Cal; Total Fat: 3 g; Saturated Fat: 1 g; Cholesterol: 12 mg; Carbohydrates: 2 g; Fiber: 0.7 g; Sugar: 2 g; Protein: 1 g;

Cinnamon Popcorn

Yield: 20 cups, 4 cups per serving

Preparation Time: 5 minutes

Cooking Time: 10 minutes

Total Time: 15 minutes

Difficulty: Level 1

MAIN INGREDIENTS:

- •4 bags of popcorns
- •1/16 teaspoon sea salt
- •8 tablespoons coconut sugar
- •2 teaspoons ground cinnamon
- •4 scoops of vanilla protein powder
- Cooking spray

DIRECTIONS:

Kid:
Pop the popcorns by following the instructions on its package, and then transfer popcorns into a large bowl.

Place cinnamon in a small bowl, add salt, sugar, and cinnamon and protein powder and then stir until mixed.

Sprinkle cinnamon mixture over the popcorns, shake well until coated, and then serve.

Nutritional Information per Serving:

Calories: 120 Cal; Total Fat: 6 g; Saturated Fat: 5 g; Cholesterol: 4 mg; Carbohydrates: 17 g; Fiber: 1 g; Sugar: 13 g; Protein: 0 g;

Popcorn Balls

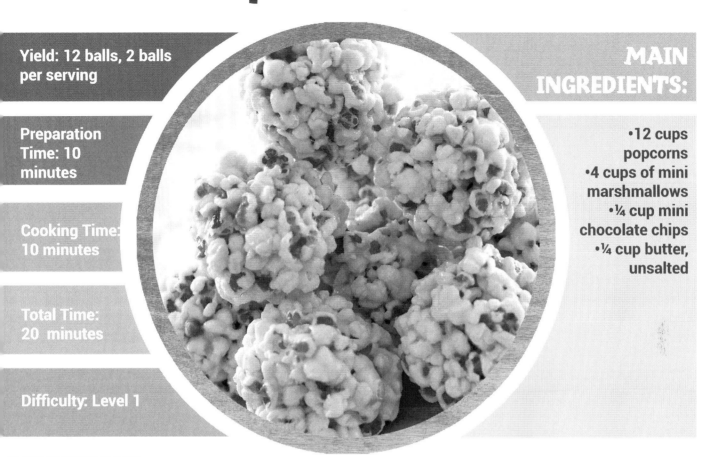

Yield: 12 balls, 2 balls per serving

Preparation Time: 10 minutes

Cooking Time: 10 minutes

Total Time: 20 minutes

Difficulty: Level 1

MAIN INGREDIENTS:

- 12 cups popcorns
- 4 cups of mini marshmallows
- ¼ cup mini chocolate chips
- ¼ cup butter, unsalted

DIRECTIONS:

Place a large saucepan over low heat, add butter and marshmallows, and then cook for 7 to 10 minutes until the marshmallows have melted, and stir continuously.

Kid:

Take a large bowl, place popcorns in it, drizzle cocoa mixture over it, mix until popcorns are fully coated, and then stir in chocolate chips until they are evenly mixed.

Take a large piece of parchment sheet, and then place it on the working space.

Adult + Kid:

Grease the hands with oil, divide popcorn mixture into twelve portions, shape each portion into a tightly packed ball, about 3-inch, and then place the popcorn ball on the piece of parchment sheet.

Let the popcorn balls rest for 10 minutes and then serve.

Nutritional Information per Serving:

Calories: 225.6 Cal; Total Fat: 6.4 g; Saturated Fat: 3.8 g; Cholesterol: 16.6 mg; Carbohydrates: 44 g; Fiber: 1.2 g; Sugar: 38.2 g; Protein: 1 g;

Deviled Eggs

Yield: 12 deviled eggs, 2 eggs per serving

Preparation Time: 10 minutes

Cooking Time: 10 minutes

Total Time: 20 minutes

Difficulty: Level 1

MAIN INGREDIENTS:

- ¼ teaspoon chopped chives
- 1 teaspoon Dijon mustard
- 1/16 teaspoon paprika
- 1 teaspoon hot sauce
- 6 eggs, at room temperature
- ¼ cup mayonnaise

Extra Ingredients:

- 1/16 teaspoon salt
- 1/16 teaspoon ground black pepper

DIRECTIONS:

Adult + Kid:
Cook the eggs until hard-boiled by following the recipe of "Hard Boiled Eggs" from the breakfast section.
Kid:
When eggs have boiled, transfer them to a bowl containing chilled water, and let them rest for 10 minutes.
Drain the eggs, peel them, cut the eggs lengthwise, and then transfer egg yolks to a bowl.
Add mustard, hot sauce, and mayonnaise, season with salt and black pepper, and then mash the egg yolks with a fork.
Spoon the yolk mixture into the egg whites, sprinkle paprika and chives over the eggs and then serve.

Nutritional Information per Serving:

Calories: 110.2 Cal; Total Fat: 5.4 g; Saturated Fat: 1.6 g; Cholesterol: 213.8 mg; Carbohydrates: 7 g; Fiber: 0.2 g; Sugar: 1.5 g; Protein: 3.3 g;

Peanut Butter Apple Rounds

Yield: 6 apple rounds, 2 rounds per serving

Preparation Time: 10 minutes

Cooking Time: 0 minutes

Total Time: 10 minutes

Difficulty: Level 1

MAIN INGREDIENTS:

- 1 medium apple
- 18 pecans
- 30 chocolate chips
- 12 almonds
- 6 tablespoons peanut butter

DIRECTIONS:

Adult + Kid:

Prepare the apple and for this, place it on a clean working space with stem-side up and then push the tip of any thin blade knife until the core ends.

Push the blade of the knife all the way through the apple, and then rotate the apple to cut the core in a circle.

Remove the knife from the apple, push the stem, separate it from the rest of the apple, and then cut the apple into six slices; the apple slices will look like a donut.

Kid:

Spread 1 tablespoon of peanut butter on one side of each apple slice, and then scatter 3 pecans and 5 chocolate chips on top.

Cut the almonds in slices, sprinkle almond slices evenly on the peanut butter layer, and then serve.

Nutritional Information per Serving:

Calories: 218 Cal; Total Fat: 8.1 g; Saturated Fat: 1.5 g; Cholesterol: 78 mg; Carbohydrates: 31.3 g; Fiber: 7.3 g; Sugar: 17.8 g; Protein: 11.6 g;

Chickpea Salad Sandwich

Yield: 4 sandwiches, 1 sandwich per serving

Preparation Time: 10 minutes

Cooking Time: 0 minutes

Total Time: 10 minutes

Difficulty: Level 1

MAIN INGREDIENTS:

- •8 slices of whole-wheat bread
- •1 can of chickpeas, about 15 ounces
- •1 stalk of celery
- •2 green onions
- •½ teaspoon minced garlic
- •1 tablespoon Dijon mustard
- •3 tablespoons mayonnaise

Extra Ingredients:

- •1/16 teaspoon salt
- •1/16 teaspoon ground black pepper
- •¼ teaspoon cayenne pepper

DIRECTIONS:

Adult + Kid:
Prepare the ingredients, and dice the celery and green onions.
Kid:
Drain the chickpeas, transfer them in a bowl, and then mash the chickpeas with a fork.
Add celery, onion, garlic, mustard, mayonnaise, salt, black pepper, and cayenne pepper, and then stir until it is well mixed.
Arrange four slices of bread on a working space, top each slice with one-fourth of the chickpea mixture, spread it evenly, and then cover with the remaining bread slices.
Serve straight away.

Nutritional Information per Serving:

Calories: 519 Cal; Total Fat: 5 g; Saturated Fat: 1 g; Cholesterol: 0 mg; Carbohydrates: 100 g; Fiber: 8 g; Sugar: 4 g; Protein: 21 g;

Mango and Banana Smoothie

Yield: 4 glasses of smoothie, 1 glass per serving

Preparation Time: 5 minutes

Cooking Time: 0 minutes

Total Time: 5 minutes

Difficulty: Level 1

MAIN INGREDIENTS:

- 1 medium mango
- 1 banana
- 2 cups orange juice
- ½ cup of ice cubes

DIRECTIONS:

Adult + Kid:
 Peel the mangoes, cut its flesh into chunks, and then remove the stones.
Kid:
 Pour orange juice in a food processor and then mango pieces.
 Peel the banana, cut it into slices, add banana slices into the food processor, and then add ice.
 Shut the food processor with its lid, and then pulse for 30 to 50 seconds until it is smooth.
 Divide the smoothie evenly among four glasses and then serve.

Nutritional Information per Serving:

Calories: 107 Cal; Total Fat: 1 g; Saturated Fat: 0 g; Cholesterol: 23 mg; Carbohydrates: 26 g; Fiber: 2 g; Sugar: 26 g; Protein: 1 g;

Peach and Mango Smoothie

Yield: 4 glasses, 1 glass per serving

Preparation Time: 5 minutes

Cooking Time: 0 minutes

Total Time: 5 minutes

Difficulty: Level 1

MAIN INGREDIENTS:

- 2 cups diced peaches, fresh
- 2 cups chopped mango
- 1 teaspoon vanilla extract, unsweetened
- 1 cup of ice cubes
- 3 cups whole milk

DIRECTIONS:

Kid:

Gather all the ingredients, and then place them in a food processor.

Cover the food processor with its lid, and then pulse for 30 to 50 seconds until smooth.

Divide the smoothie among four glasses and then serve.

Nutritional Information per Serving:

Calories: 115 Cal; Total Fat: 2.5 g; Saturated Fat: 0.1 g; Cholesterol: 0 mg; Carbohydrates: 22.3 g; Fiber: 1.3 g; Sugar: 18.1 g; Protein: 2.5 g;

Flax Muffin

Yield: 1 muffin

Preparation Time: 5 minutes

Cooking Time: 1 minutes

Total Time: 6 minutes

Difficulty: Level 1

MAIN INGREDIENTS:

- ¼ cup flaxseed meal
- ½ teaspoon baking powder
- ¼ teaspoon stevia powder
- 1 teaspoon ground cinnamon
- 1 egg, at room temperature
- 1 teaspoon olive oil

DIRECTIONS:

Kid:

Take a coffee mug, place all the ingredients in it, and then stir until mixed.

Place the mug in the microwave oven and then cook for 1 minute at a high heat setting.

Top with some butter and then serve.

Nutritional Information per Serving:

Calories: 268 Cal; Total Fat: 21.1 g; Saturated Fat: 3.2 g; Cholesterol: 186 mg; Carbohydrates: 11.1 g; Fiber: 9 g; Sugar: 0.7 g; Protein: 11.5 g;

Black Bean and Corn Salad

Yield: 4 bowls, 1 bowl per serving

Preparation Time: 10 minutes

Cooking Time: 0 minutes

Total Time: 20 minutes

Difficulty: Level 1

MAIN INGREDIENTS:

- 1 can of black beans, about 15 ounces
- 1 medium white onion
- 1 medium tomato
- 2 tablespoons minced cilantro
- 2 cups canned corn kernels
- ¼ teaspoon minced garlic
- 2 tablespoons lemon juice
- 3 tablespoons olive oil

Extra Ingredients:

- ¼ teaspoon salt
- ¼ teaspoon ground black pepper

DIRECTIONS:

Adult + Kid:
 Peel the onion, chop it and then chop the tomato.
Kid:
 Drain the beans and corn, rinse well and then drain well.
 Place beans and corn in a medium bowl, add garlic, and then stir until mixed.
 Pour lemon juice in a small bowl, stir in oil, pour this mixture over the bean mixture and then stir until combined.
 Add salt and black pepper, add cilantro and then stir until combined.
 Serve straight away.

Nutritional Information per Serving:

Calories: 279.4 Cal; Total Fat: 11.7 g; Saturated Fat: 1.6 g; Cholesterol: 0 mg; Carbohydrates: 37.3 g; Fiber: 9.4 g; Sugar: 3.8 g; Protein: 10.2 g;

Fruit Pizza

Yield: 6 wedges, 2 wedges per serving

Preparation Time: 5 minutes

Cooking Time: 0 minutes

Total Time: 5 minutes

Difficulty: Level 1

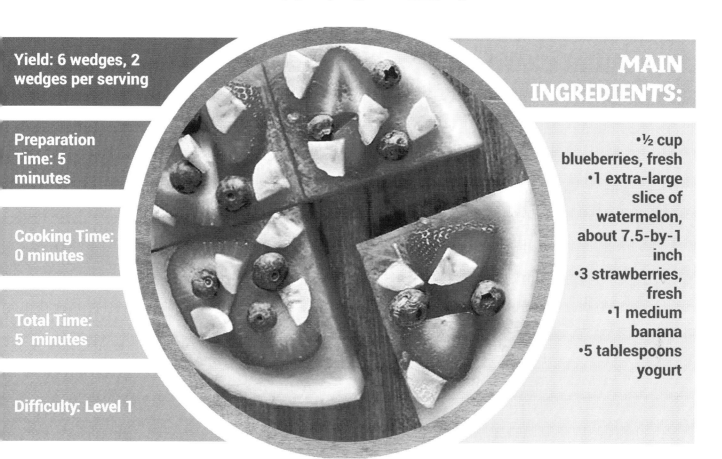

MAIN INGREDIENTS:

- ½ cup blueberries, fresh
- 1 extra-large slice of watermelon, about 7.5-by-1 inch
- 3 strawberries, fresh
- 1 medium banana
- 5 tablespoons yogurt

DIRECTIONS:

Place the watermelon on a cutting board and then cut it into 6 wedges.

Peel and slice the banana, and then cut each strawberry in half.

Spoon 1 tablespoon of yogurt on each watermelon wedge, spread it evenly, and then top with strawberry halves, some blueberries, and some banana slices.

Serve straight away.

Nutritional Information per Serving:

Calories: 61 Cal; Total Fat: 0.7 g; Saturated Fat: 0.3 g; Cholesterol: 0 mg; Carbohydrates: 12 g; Fiber: 1.4 g; Sugar: 9 g; Protein: 1.2 g;

Chapter 7: Dessert
List of Kid-Friendly Foods for Dessert

Strawberry – Sweet, beautiful, and nutritious; strawberries are among the best fruits children can eat. They are especially rich in Vitamin C that helps them fight germs and stay healthy.

Raspberries – Raspberries are different from other fruits by having more amounts of folic acid and zinc in them. They are also vibrant in color and filled with antioxidants.

Blackberries – Antioxidants are chemicals that keep cancer cells from growing. Blackberries are one of the best sources of them. They are sweet and filled with germ-fighting Vitamin C too.

Pear – A healthy diet contains different types of fruits. Pears are rich in fiber, and it keeps blood sugar levels in control.

Oranges – Every kid loves oranges. It is one of the richest sources of Vitamin C and also provides flavonoids. They are far superior to any fruit juice you can buy from the store.

Apples – Apples are rich in iron and antioxidants, and they help improve our eyes. They are especially good for people who have asthma.

Cantaloupe – It is a good idea to add a different color of fruits on your plate from time to time. Cantaloupe has Vitamin A, C, and folacin. They help prevent anemia as well.

Honeydew – It is a type of melon that is rich in Vitamin C and different minerals. They are good for bones and skin.

Pineapple – It is delicious and great for our immune system. Pineapple helps to build our bones and also aid in indigestion. Good amounts of antioxidants are present as well.

Dried apricot – It removes bad cholesterol and introduces good cholesterol that keeps your heart happy. Apricots also keep our electrolytes balanced.

Mango – One of the most delicious ingredients, mangoes are good for your eyesight, memory, and skin. They are beneficial for maintaining a healthy weight and a good digestion system.

Chocolate – You think chocolate would be bad for you, but actually, it promotes brain growth and helps in developing problem-solving skills.

Rainbow Fruit Kabobs

Yield: 4 skewers, 4 skewers per serving

Preparation Time: 5 minutes

Cooking Time: 0 minutes

Total Time: 5 minutes

Difficulty: Level 1

MAIN INGREDIENTS:

- 4 raspberries
- 4 cubes of cantaloupe
- 4 cubes of pineapple
- 4 cubes of mango
- 8 blueberries
- 4 slices of kiwi
- 4 wooden skewer

DIRECTIONS:

Kid:

Take a wooden skewer, thread a raspberry, thread a cube of cantaloupe, pineapple, mango, and kiwi and then thread two blueberries at the end.

Prepare three more fruit skewers in the same manner and then serve.

Nutritional Information per Serving:

Calories: 30.4 Cal; Total Fat: 0.2 g; Saturated Fat: 0.02 g; Cholesterol: 0 mg; Carbohydrates: 6.8 g; Fiber: 1.1 g; Sugar: 6.1 g; Protein: 0.4 g;

Fruit Popsicles

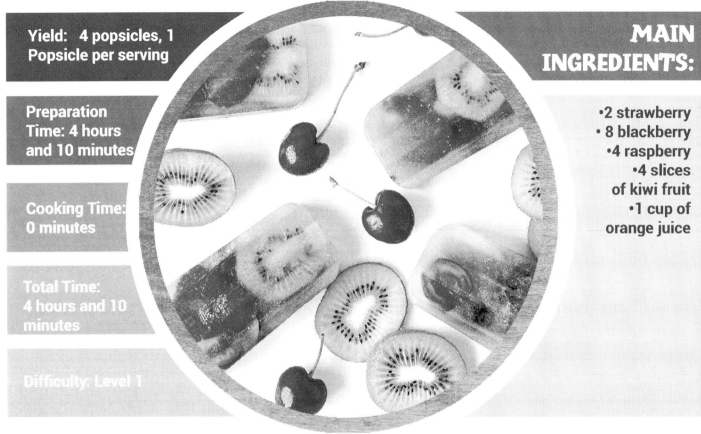

Yield: 4 popsicles, 1 Popsicle per serving

Preparation Time: 4 hours and 10 minutes

Cooking Time: 0 minutes

Total Time: 4 hours and 10 minutes

Difficulty: Level 1

MAIN INGREDIENTS:

- •2 strawberry
- • 8 blackberry
- •4 raspberry
- •4 slices of kiwi fruit
- •1 cup of orange juice

DIRECTIONS:

Adult + Kid:

Cut the strawberries in half, take four Popsicle mold, and then place the strawberry halves in it, with one strawberry half per mold.

Kid:

Add 2 blackberries, 1 raspberry, and 1 slice of kiwi fruit into each mold and then nestle a Popsicle stick into the bottom center of each milk.

Pour ¼ cup of orange juice into each mold and freeze for a minimum of 4 hours until set.

When you are done, let the popsicles stand for 5 minutes, at room temperature, and then lift them out and serve.

Nutritional Information per Serving:

Calories: 51 Cal; Total Fat: 0 g; Saturated Fat: 0 g; Cholesterol: 0 mg; Carbohydrates: 12 g; Fiber: 1.7 g; Sugar 10 g; Protein: 1 g;

Glazed Pears

Yield: 12 servings, 1 pear per serving

Preparation Time: 10 minutes

Cooking Time: 25 minutes

Total Time: 35 minutes

Difficulty: Level 1

MAIN INGREDIENTS:

- •12 pears
- •4 tablespoons brown sugar
- •2 lemons, juiced
- •2 tablespoons butter, unsalted
- •2 cups of water

DIRECTIONS:

Kid:
 Juice the lemons in a medium bowl, pour in water, and then stir until mixed.
Adult + Kid:
 Cut each pear in half and then core it.
Kid:
 Add pear halves into the bowl containing lemon water, and let them soak for 10 minutes.
 Drain the pear halves and then pat dry with paper towels.
Adult:
 Place a large skillet pan over medium heat, add butter, and let it melt.
Adult + Kid:
 Add pears and then cook for 10 minutes until pear pieces start to release their juices.
 Sprinkle sugar over the pear halves, and continue cooking for 10 to 15 minutes, until the pear halves have glazed.
 Serve straight away.

Nutritional Information per Serving:

 Calories: 164.6 Cal; Total Fat: 2.2 g; Saturated Fat: 1.2 g; Cholesterol: 5.1 mg; Carbohydrates: 39.4 g; Fiber: 5.9 g; Sugar: 26.3 g; Protein: 1 g;

Apple Chips

Yield: 4

Preparation Time: 10 minutes

Cooking Time: 24 minutes

Total Time: 34 minutes

Difficulty: Level 1

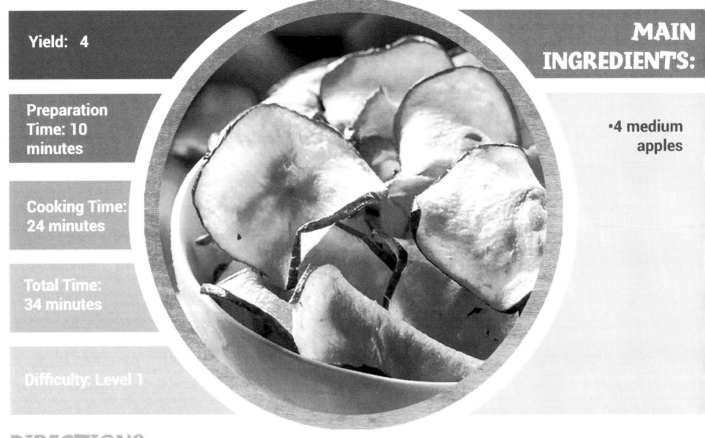

MAIN INGREDIENTS:

- 4 medium apples

DIRECTIONS:

Adult + Kid:

Prepare the apple and for this, place it on a clean working space with stem-side up, and then push the tip o any thin blade knife until the core ends.

Push the blade of the knife all the way through the apple, and then rotate the apple to cut the core in a circle.

Remove the knife from the apple, push the stem, separate it from the rest of the apple, and then cut the apple into thin slices; the apple slices will look like a donut.

Kid:

Take a heatproof plate, line it with parchment paper, and then spread some apple slices on a single layer.

Place the apple into the microwave oven and then heat for 5 minutes until the edges of the apple begin to curl.

Flip the apple slices and continue microwaving for 1 minute until the edges of apple slices are completely crisp.

When you are done, let the apple chips stand for 10 minutes until dry and crisp, and then repeat with the remaining apple slices.

Serve immediately.

Nutritional Information per Serving:

Calories: 94 Cal; Total Fat: 0 g; Saturated Fat: 0 g; Cholesterol: 0 mg; Carbohydrates: 25 g; Fiber: 4 g; Sugar: 18 g; Protein: 0 g;

Vanilla Cupcakes

Yield: 12 cupcakes, 2 cupcakes per serving

Preparation Time: 10 minutes

Cooking Time: 20 minutes

Total Time: 30 minutes

Difficulty: Level 2

MAIN INGREDIENTS:

- 1 ½ cups white all-purpose flour
- 1 ½ teaspoon baking powder
- 2 teaspoons vanilla extract, unsweetened
- ½ cup butter, unsalted, at room temperature
- 2 eggs, at room temperature
- ¾ cup whole-milk

Extra Ingredients:
- ½ teaspoon salt
- 1 cup of sugar

DIRECTIONS:

Adult:
Switch on the oven, then set it to 350 degrees F, and let it preheat.
Kid:
Take 12 muffin cups and then line its cups with a muffin liner.
Place flour in a medium bowl, add salt and baking powder, and then stir until mixed.
Adult + Kid:
Take a separate medium bowl, add butter, and then beat in sugar until fluffy.
Beat in eggs, one at a time, and then beat in vanilla until combined.
Add ½ cup of the flour mixture into the egg, beat it until incorporated, and then beat in remaining flour, ½ cup at a time until a smooth batter comes together.
Spoon the batter evenly among 12 muffin cups until each cup is two-third full, and then bake them for 18 to 20 minutes until the top turns golden brown.
When you are done, transfer the cupcakes to the wire rack, let them cool completely, and then serve.

Nutritional Information per Serving:

Calories: 460 Cal; Total Fat: 19 g; Saturated Fat: 11 g; Cholesterol: 16 mg; Carbohydrates: 70 g; Fiber: 0 g; Sugar: 57 g; Protein: 3 g;

Yogurt Bowl with Berries

Yield: 4

Preparation Time: 10 minutes

Cooking Time: 24 minutes

Total Time: 34 minutes

Difficulty: Level 1

MAIN INGREDIENTS:

- ½ cup raspberries, fresh
- ½ cup blueberries, fresh
- ½ cup blackberries, fresh
- 2 tablespoons honey
- 2 cups yogurt

DIRECTIONS:

Kid:
Divide yogurt evenly between two bowls, 1 cup yogurt per bowl.
Add ¼ cup each of berries into each yogurt bowl, and then drizzle 1 tablespoon honey on top.
Serve immediately.

Nutritional Information per Serving:

Calories: 268 Cal; Total Fat: 8.3 g; Saturated Fat: 5.2 g; Cholesterol: 8 mg; Carbohydrates: 37.9 g; Fiber: 4.8 g; Sugar: 35.6 g; Protein: 9.9 g;

Chocolate Covered Strawberries

Yield: 20 berries, 4 berries per serving

Preparation Time: 10 minutes

Cooking Time: 20 minutes

Total Time: 30 minutes

Difficulty: Level 1

MAIN INGREDIENTS:

- •20 large strawberries, fresh
- •½ cup dark chocolate, semi-sweet
- •¼ cup sprinkles

DIRECTIONS:

Adult + Kid:

Chop the chocolate, place it in a small heatproof bowl, and then microwave for 30 seconds.

Stir the chocolate and if it hasn't melted, microwave it for another 30 seconds.

Kid:

Take a shallow dish, and spread sprinkles in it.

Take a plate, and then line it with a parchment sheet.

Take a strawberry, pick it from its stem, dip the berry into melted chocolate, and then roll into sprinkle until coated.

Place the coated strawberry on the prepared plate, and then repeat with the remaining berries.

Serve straight away.

Nutritional Information per Serving:

Calories: 280 Cal; Total Fat: 14 g; Saturated Fat: 4 g; Cholesterol: 0 mg; Carbohydrates: 36 g; Fiber: 2 g; ugar: 12 g; Protein: 4 g;

Fudge

Yield: 8 squares, 2 squares per serving

Preparation Time: 10 minutes

Cooking Time: 3 minutes

Total Time: 13 minutes

Difficulty: Level 1

MAIN INGREDIENTS:

- 3 cups chocolate chips, semi-sweet
- ¼ cup butter, unsalted
- 1 can of condensed milk, sweetened, about 14 ounces

DIRECTIONS:

Kid:

Place chocolate chips in a heatproof bowl, add butter and milk, and then microwave it for 1 minute and 30 seconds.

Stir the chocolate chips, continue microwaving for 1 minute and 30 seconds, and then stir until smooth.

Adult + Kid:

Take a square glass baking dish, about 8-by-8 inches, pour the fudge mixture in it and then smooth the top with a spatula.

Place the baking dish into the refrigerator, and let the fudge chill for 2 hours until set.

Then cut the fudge into 1-by-1 inch squares and serve.

Nutritional Information per Serving:

Calories: 140 Cal; Total Fat: 3.6 g; Saturated Fat: 2.2 g; Cholesterol: 4 mg; Carbohydrates: 26 g; Fiber: 0.6 g; Sugar: 24.8 g; Protein: 0.8 g;

Strawberry Soup

Yield: 6 bowls, 1 bowl per serving

Preparation Time: 10 minutes

Cooking Time: 0 minutes

Total Time: 10 minutes

Difficulty: Level 1

MAIN INGREDIENTS:

- 8 cups strawberries, fresh
- ½ cup of sugar
- 2 cups yogurt, vanilla flavor
- ½ cup of orange juice

DIRECTIONS:

Place all the ingredients in a food processor, and then pulse for 1 to 2 minutes until blended and smooth. Divide the soup evenly among six bowls, chill the soup in the refrigerator for a minimum of 2 hours, and then serve.

Nutritional Information per Serving:

Calories: 192 Cal; Total Fat: 1 g; Saturated Fat: 1 g; Cholesterol: 4 mg; Carbohydrates: 42 g; Fiber: 3 g; Sugar: 37 g; Protein: 5 g;

Strawberry Shortcake Smoothie

Yield: 3 glasses, 1 glass per serving

Preparation Time: 5 minutes

Cooking Time: 0 minutes

Total Time: 5 minutes

Difficulty: Level 1

MAIN INGREDIENTS:

- 2 cups strawberries, fresh or frozen
- 4 dates, pitted
- 6 shortbread cookies
- 6 tablespoons whey protein powder
- 1 teaspoon vanilla extract, unsweetened
- 2 cups yogurt
- 2 cups whole milk

DIRECTIONS:

Kid:

Gather all the ingredients and then place them in a food processor.

Cover the food processor with its lid, and then pulse for 30 to 50 seconds until it is smooth.

Divide the smoothie among three glasses and then serve.

Nutritional Information per Serving:

Calories: 361 Cal; Total Fat: 8.7 g; Saturated Fat: 3 g; Cholesterol: 18.8 mg; Carbohydrates: 39.5 g; Fiber: 2.2 g; Sugar: 28.8 g; Protein: 33 g;

Black Forest Smoothie

Yield: 1 glass, 1 glass per serving

Preparation Time: 10 minutes

Cooking Time: 0 minutes

Total Time: 10 minutes

Difficulty: Level 1

MAIN INGREDIENTS:

- ¼ cup rolled oats
- 1 cup frozen cherries
- 1 cup baby spinach
- 2 Medjool dates, pitted
- 2 tablespoons cocoa powder, unsweetened
- 1 tablespoon chia seeds
- 1 cup whole milk, unsweetened

DIRECTIONS:

Kid:

Gather all the ingredients, and then place them in a food processor.

Cover the food processor with its lid, and then pulse for 30 to 50 seconds until it is smooth.

Divide the smoothie among three glasses and then serve.

Nutritional Information per Serving:

Calories: 456 Cal; Total Fat: 9.2 g; Saturated Fat: 1.8 g; Cholesterol: 0 mg; Carbohydrates: 72.4 g; Fiber: 18.3 g; Sugar: 36 g; Protein: 28.4 g;

Chocolate and Lentil Muffins

Yield: 12 muffins, 2 muffins per serving

Preparation Time: 10 minutes

Cooking Time: 15 minutes

Total Time: 25 minutes

Difficulty: Level 1

MAIN INGREDIENTS:

- 1 large banana, peeled
- 1 cup canned red lentils, drained
- 1/3 cup cocoa powder, unsweetened
- 1/3 cup dark chocolate chips
- 3 tablespoons coconut oil
- 3 eggs, at room temperature

Extra Ingredients:

- 1 teaspoon baking soda
- 1 teaspoon vanilla extract, unsweetened
- ¼ cup honey

DIRECTIONS:

Adult:

Switch on the oven, then set it to 350 degrees F, and let it preheat.

Meanwhile, take a 12-cup muffin tray and then line the muffin cups with its liners.

Kid:

Place banana into a food processor, add lentils, baking soda, cocoa powder, honey, vanilla, and coconut oil, and then pulse for 30 to 40 seconds until smooth.

Spoon the batter into a bowl, and then stir in chocolate chips with a wooden spoon until mixed.

Adult + Kid:

Spoon the batter into muffin cups until each cup has two-third full, and then bake them for 10 to 15 minutes until firm.

When you are done, transfer muffins to a wire rack and then serve.

Nutritional Information per Serving:

Calories: 234 Cal; Total Fat: 11 g; Saturated Fat: 3 g; Cholesterol: 78 mg; Carbohydrates: 34 g; Fiber: 4 g; Sugar: 18 g; Protein: 3 g;

Fruit Salad

Yield: 1

Preparation Time: 5 minutes

Cooking Time: 0 minutes

Total Time: 5 minutes

Difficulty: Level 1

MAIN INGREDIENTS:

- 1 kiwi
- ¼ cup strawberries, fresh
- ¼ cup mango chunks
- ¼ cup blueberries
- ¼ cup blackberries
- ¼ cup grapes
- 1 lemon

Extra Ingredients:

- ½ teaspoon honey

DIRECTIONS:

Kid:

Juice the lemon in a small bowl and then stir in honey.

Adult + Kid:

Peel and slice the kiwi, and then add it into a salad bowl.

Cut strawberries into half, add to the salad bowl, and then add mango, grapes, blueberries, and blackberries.

Kid:

Drizzle with lemon-honey mixture, toss until coated, chill the salad in the refrigerator for 30 minutes, and then serve.

Nutritional Information per Serving:

Calories: 133 Cal; Total Fat: 1 g; Saturated Fat: 0.2 g; Cholesterol: 0 mg; Carbohydrates: 33 g; Fiber: 6 g; Sugar: 23 g; Protein: 2 g;

Pineapple and Yogurt Dip

Yield: 4 servings

Preparation Time: 5 minutes

Cooking Time: 0 minutes

Total Time: 5 minutes

Difficulty: Level 1

MAIN INGREDIENTS:

- 8 ounces of canned crushed pineapple
- 12 ounces of yogurt

DIRECTIONS:

Drain the pineapple, place the pineapple chunks in a food processor, and then add yogurt.
Pulse for 40 to 60 seconds until smooth, and then spoon the dip into a bowl.
Top with some more pineapple chunks, and then serve it with your favorite fruit slices.

Nutritional Information per Serving:

Calories: 150 Cal; Total Fat: 5 g; Saturated Fat: 3.5 g; Cholesterol: 25 mg; Carbohydrates: 17 g; Fiber: 0 g; Sugar: 15 g; Protein: 9 g;

Banana Popsicles

Yield: 1

Preparation Time: 10 minutes

Cooking Time: 0 minutes

Total Time: 10 minutes

Difficulty: Level 1

MAIN INGREDIENTS:

- 2 banana
- ¼ cup almonds
- ½ cup yogurt

DIRECTIONS:

Adult + Kid:

   Chop the almonds, and then place them in a shallow dish.

Adult:

   Take a separate shallow dish and place yogurt in it.

   Take a plate and then line it with a parchment sheet.

   Peel a banana, insert a Popsicle stick in it, and then use it to roll the banana in the yogurt until completely coated.

   Then roll the banana into chopped almonds until coated, and place onto the prepared plate.

   Repeat with the other banana, then freeze the bananas for 30 minutes, until firm, and then serve.

Nutritional Information per Serving:

Calories: 237 Cal; Total Fat: 9.9 g; Saturated Fat: 2 g; Cholesterol: 207 mg; Carbohydrates: 30.2 g; Fiber: 5.1 g; Sugar: 18 g; Protein: 6.5 g;

Grilled Vegetables

Yield: 4 packets, 1 packet per serving

Preparation Time: 10 minutes

Cooking Time: 20 minutes

Total Time: 30 minutes

Difficulty: Level 1

MAIN INGREDIENTS:

- 4 medium carrots
- 4 medium red onions
- 4 medium potatoes
- 2 cups broccoli florets
- 4 tablespoons olive oil

Extra Ingredients:

- 1 ½ teaspoon salt
- 1 teaspoon ground black pepper
- 1 ½ teaspoon paprika

DIRECTIONS:

Set the grill, and then let it preheat at medium heat setting.

Meanwhile, prepare the vegetables and for this, peel the onion, and then cut them into chunks.

Peel the carrots, cut each carrot in half, and then cut each half into three pieces.

Peel the potatoes and then cut it into wedges.

Place all the vegetables in a large bowl, add oil, salt, black pepper, and paprika and then toss until coated.

Cut out eight pieces of foil sheets, each piece about 12-by-18 inches, and then distribute vegetables evenly in the center of four foil pieces.

Cover vegetables with another sheet of foil, and then fold up all the edges tightly.

Adult:

Then place the vegetable packets on the grill, and then cook the vegetables for 20 minutes, and turn the packets after 10 minutes.

When you are done, let the vegetables rest for 5 minutes, then open the packets and serve.

Nutritional Information per Serving:

Calories: 347.7 Cal; Total Fat: 13.5 g; Saturated Fat: 1.9 g; Cholesterol: 230 mg; Carbohydrates: 51.3 g; Fiber: 9.4 g; Sugar: 10.5 g; Protein: 5.2 g;

Cheesy Fries

Yield: 4 packets, 1 packet per serving

Preparation Time: 10 minutes

Cooking Time: 22 minutes

Total Time: 32 minutes

Difficulty: Level 1

MAIN INGREDIENTS:

- 4 tablespoons cooked bacon bits
- 2 medium green onions, chopped
- 1 bag of French fries, about 14 ounces
- 4 slices of cheese
- 2 tablespoons butter, unsalted

DIRECTIONS:

Set the grill. and then let it preheat at medium-high heat setting.

Meanwhile, take a large heatproof bowl, add butter in it, and then microwave it for 1 minute until butter melts.

Add fries into the melted butter and toss with a tong until coated.

Cut out two pieces of aluminum foil, each piece about a 12-by-8 inch, and then place half of the fries in the center of each foil piece.

Fold the edge of the foil to form a boat, place the potato fries boats on the grill grate, and then shut the grill.

Cook the fries for 20 minutes until crisp, stirring fries halfway and when done, top each packet of fries with 2 slices of cheese.

Continue cooking the fries for 2 minutes until the cheese melts and, when done, sprinkle 2 tablespoons of bacon on top of each potato fries packet and chopped green onions.

Serve straight away.

Nutritional Information per Serving:

Calories: 260 Cal; Total Fat: 15 g; Saturated Fat: 6 g; Cholesterol: 35 mg; Carbohydrates: 22 g; Fiber: 2 g; Sugar: 2 g; Protein: 8 g;

Lemon and Parmesan Broccoli

Yield: 1

Preparation Time: 10 minutes

Cooking Time: 0 minutes

Total Time: 10 minutes

Difficulty: Level 1

MAIN INGREDIENTS:

- 1 bag of broccoli florets, about 12 ounces
- ½ teaspoon salt ¼ teaspoon ground black pepper
- 2 tablespoons lemon juice
- 2 tablespoons olive oil
- 4 tablespoons grated parmesan cheese

DIRECTIONS:

Set the grill, and then let it preheat at medium-high heat setting.

Meanwhile, cut out two pieces of aluminum foil, each piece about a 12-by-8 inch, and then place half of the broccoli florets in the center of each foil piece.

Drizzle 1 tablespoon oil and lemon juice over each portion of florets, and then sprinkle ¼ teaspoon salt and 1/8 teaspoon black pepper over the top.

Bring the edges of foil together, seal the edges on each side by folding them, and then place the packets over the grilling rack.

Shut the grill and then cook the broccoli florets for 20 minutes until through hot, turning halfway.

Remove packets from the grill, open them carefully and then sprinkle parmesan cheese over the top.

Serve straight away.

Nutritional Information per Serving:

Calories: 140 Cal; Total Fat: 10 g; Saturated Fat: 2.5 g; Cholesterol: 5 mg; Carbohydrates: 7 g; Fiber: 3 g; Sugar: 2 g; Protein: 7 g;

Shrimp Boil

Yield: 4 packets, 1 packet per serving

Preparation Time: 10 minutes

Cooking Time: 10 minutes

Total Time: 20 minutes

Difficulty: Level 1

MAIN INGREDIENTS:

- 1 pound shrimps, peeled, deveined
- 3 ears of corn, quartered
- ½ pound smoked sausage, 1-inch sliced
- 1 tablespoon minced garlic
- 2 tablespoons chopped cilantro
- 2 lemons, juiced
- 4 tablespoons butter, unsalted

Extra Ingredients:

- 1 ½ teaspoon salt
- ¾ teaspoon ground black pepper
- 2 tablespoons olive oil
- 1 teaspoon red pepper flakes

DIRECTIONS:

Set the grill, and then let it preheat at a high heat setting.

Meanwhile, place shrimps in a large bowl, add remaining ingredients except for butter, and then toss until combined.

Cut out four pieces of aluminum foil, each piece about 12-inch, and then evenly distribute shrimp mixture in the center of each foil piece.

Top 1 tablespoon butter on top of shrimp mixture, bring the edges of foil together, seal the edges on each side by folding them and then place the packets over the grilling rack.

Shut the grill and then cook for 10 minutes until shrimps have turned pink, turning halfway.

Serve straight away.

Nutritional Information per Serving:

Calories: 382.2 Cal; Total Fat: 11.6 g; Saturated Fat: 3.6 g; Cholesterol: 156.3 mg; Carbohydrates: 29.4 g; Fiber: 4 g; Sugar: 4 g; Protein: 28.9 g;

Lemon and Dijon Salmon

Yield: 4 packets, 1 packet per serving

Preparation Time: 10 minutes

Cooking Time: 15 minutes

Total Time: 25 minutes

Difficulty: Level 1

MAIN INGREDIENTS:

- 4 salmon fillets, each about 4 ounces
- 1 tablespoon capers, drained
- 1 tablespoon minced garlic
- 1/2 teaspoon dill weed
- 4 teaspoons lemon juice
- 4 teaspoons olive oil
- 1 tablespoon Dijon mustard

Extra Ingredients:

- 1/4 teaspoon salt
- 1/8 teaspoon cayenne pepper
- 1/2 teaspoon dried thyme

DIRECTIONS:

Set the grill, and then let it preheat at a high heat setting.

Meanwhile, cut out four pieces of aluminum foil, each piece about a 12-by-8 inch, and then place a salmon fillet in the center of each foil piece.

Place remaining ingredients in a small bowl, stir until combined, and then spoon over salmon fillets.

Bring the edges of foil together, and then seal the edges on each side by folding them, and then place the packets over the grilling rack.

Shut the grill, and then cook the salmon for 15 minutes until fillets turn fork-tender, turning halfway.

Serve straight away.

Nutritional Information per Serving:

Calories: 225 Cal; Total Fat: 15 g; Saturated Fat: 3 g; Cholesterol: 359 mg; Carbohydrates: 2 g; Fiber: 0 g; Sugar: 0 g; Protein: 19 g;

Lemon Garlic Shrimps

Yield: 4 packets, 1 packet per serving

Preparation Time: 10 minutes

Cooking Time: 10 minutes

Total Time: 20 minutes

Difficulty: Level 1

MAIN INGREDIENTS:

- 1 pound shrimps, peeled, deveined
- 1 ½ tablespoon minced garlic
- 1 teaspoon lemon zest
- 1 teaspoon dried parsley
- 1 tablespoon lemon juice
- 4 tablespoons butter, unsalted

Extra Ingredients:

- 1/8 teaspoon salt
- ¼ teaspoon red pepper flakes

DIRECTIONS:

Set the grill and then let it preheat at a high heat setting.

Meanwhile, cut out four pieces of aluminum foil, each piece about a 12-by-8 inch, and then place shrimps in the center of each foil piece.

Place remaining ingredients in a small bowl, stir until combined, and then spoon over shrimps.

Bring the edges of foil together, and then seal the edges on each side by folding them, and then place the packets over the grilling rack.

Shut the grill and then cook for 15 minutes until shrimps have turned pink, turning halfway.

Serve straight away.

Nutritional Information per Serving:

Calories: 340 Cal; Total Fat: 22 g; Saturated Fat: 6 g; Cholesterol: 280 mg; Carbohydrates: 2 g; Fiber: 0.5 g; Sugar: 2 g; Protein: 24 g;

Corn on the Cob

Yield: 4 packets, 1 packet per serving

Preparation Time: 10 minutes

Cooking Time: 20 minutes

Total Time: 30 minutes

Difficulty: Level 1

MAIN INGREDIENTS:

- 4 ears of sweet corn, husk removed
- 2 tablespoons horseradish
- ½ tablespoon dried parsley
- ¼ teaspoon dried thyme
- 1 teaspoon vinegar
- 4 tablespoons butter, unsalted
- 2 tablespoons shredded pepper jack cheese

Extra Ingredients:

- 1 ½ teaspoon salt
- ¼ teaspoon ground black pepper

DIRECTIONS:

Set the grill and then let it preheat at medium heat setting.

Meanwhile, cut out four pieces of aluminum foil, each piece about a 12-by-8 inch, and then place corn in the center of each foil piece.

Place remaining ingredients in a small bowl, stir until combined, and then spoon over the corns.

Wrap the foil around the corns, seal the edges on each side by folding them, and then place the packets over the grilling rack.

Shut the grill and then cook for 20 minutes until the corn has cooked, turning halfway.

Serve straight away.

Nutritional Information per Serving:

Calories: 203 Cal; Total Fat: 14 g; Saturated Fat: 8 g; Cholesterol: 33 mg; Carbohydrates: 20 g; Fiber: 2 g; Sugar: 7 g; Protein: 4 g;

Sriracha Honey Wings

Yield: 4 packets, 1 packet per serving

Preparation Time: 10 minutes

Cooking Time: 30 minutes

Total Time: 40 minutes

Difficulty: Level 1

MAIN INGREDIENTS:

- 1 pound chicken wings
- 4 teaspoons sesame seeds
- 2 tablespoons honey
- 2 tablespoons apple cider vinegar
- 4 tablespoons Sriracha sauce
- 2 tablespoons soy sauce
- 4 teaspoons sesame oil

DIRECTIONS:

Take a large plastic bag, place all the ingredients in it, and then seal the bag.

Turn the bag upside down until chicken wings have coated, and then let the chicken wings marinate for a minimum of 30 minutes in the refrigerator.

Then set the grill and then let it preheat at medium-high heat setting.

Meanwhile, cut out four pieces of aluminum foil, each piece about a 12-by-8 inch, and then place chicken wings in the center of each foil piece.

Bring the edges of foil together, and then seal the edges on each side by folding them, and then place the packets over the grilling rack.

Shut the grill and then cook for 30 minutes until chicken wings have cooked, turning halfway.

Serve straight away.

Nutritional Information per Serving:

Calories: 570 Cal; Total Fat: 27 g; Saturated Fat: 3 g; Cholesterol: 75 mg; Carbohydrates: 54 g; Fiber: 3 g; Sugar: 12 g; Protein: 30 g;

Hash Browns

Preparation Time: 5 minutes

Cooking Time: 15 minutes

Total Time: 20 minutes

Difficulty: Level 1

MAIN INGREDIENTS:

- 3 ½ cups cubed hash brown potatoes, thawed
- ¼ teaspoon seasoned salt
- 1 small white onion, peeled, chopped
- ¼ teaspoon ground black pepper
- 1 tablespoon butter, unsalted, melted

DIRECTIONS:

Set the grill, and then let it preheat at medium heat setting.
Meanwhile, cut out a 10-by-18 inches piece of aluminum foil and then potatoes in the center.
Season with salt and black pepper, add onion, drizzle with butter, and then
Bring the edges of foil together, and then seal the edges on each side by folding them, and then place the packet over the grilling rack.
Shut the grill, and then cook for 15 minutes until potatoes have cooked, turning halfway.
Serve straight away.

Nutritional Information per Serving:

Calories: 89 Cal; Total Fat: 3 g; Saturated Fat: 2 g; Cholesterol: 8 mg; Carbohydrates: 14 g; Fiber: 1 g; Sugar: 2 g; Protein: 2 g;

Green Beans

Yield: 1 packet, ¼ of a packet per serving

Preparation Time: 10 minutes

Cooking Time: 20 minutes

Total Time: 30 minutes

Difficulty: Level 1

MAIN INGREDIENTS:

- 1 small shallot, peeled, minced
- 1 pound fresh green beans, trimmed
- ½ teaspoon minced garlic
- 2 tablespoons butter, unsalted
- ½ cup grated Parmesan cheese
- 4 quarts water

DIRECTIONS:

Set the grill and then let it preheat at medium-high heat setting.

Meanwhile, pour water in a large pot, place it over high heat and then bring it to a boil.

Add green beans, cook for 3 minutes until beans turn tender-crisp, and then immediately transfer green beans into a bowl containing ice-chilled water

Place butter in a small skillet pan, place it over medium-high heat, and let it melt.

Add shallot, cook it for 3 minutes, stir in garlic and continue cooking for 30 seconds, set aside until required.

Drain the green beans, pat them dry, and transfer in a large bowl.

Add shallow mixture, add cheese, and then toss until well coated.

Meanwhile, cut out an 18-by-18 inches piece of aluminum foil and then green beans in the center.

Bring the edges of foil together, and then seal the edges on each side by folding them, and then place the packet over the grilling rack.

Shut the grill and then cook for 10 minutes until green beans have cooked, turning halfway.

Serve straight away.

Nutritional Information per Serving:

Calories: 137 Cal; Total Fat: 9 g; Saturated Fat: 5 g; Cholesterol: 24 mg; Carbohydrates: 12 g; Fiber: 4 g; Sugar: 3 g; Protein: 5 g;

Philly Cheesesteak

Yield: packets, 1 packet per serving

Preparation Time: 10 minutes

Cooking Time: 10 minutes

Total Time: 20 minutes

Difficulty: Level 1

MAIN INGREDIENTS:

- 1 pound steak, sliced
- ½ of a medium white onion, peeled, sliced
- 1 tablespoon minced garlic
- 2 medium green bell pepper, cored, sliced
- 2 tablespoons Italian seasoning
- 4 slices of provolone cheese
- 2 tablespoons olive oil

Extra Ingredients:

- 1 teaspoon salt
- ½ teaspoon ground black pepper

DIRECTIONS:

Set the grill and then let it preheat at medium-high heat setting.

Meanwhile, place steak slices in a large bowl, add onion, bell pepper, and garlic, drizzle with oil, season with black pepper and salt and then toss until coated.

Meanwhile, cut out four pieces of aluminum foil, each piece about a 12-by-8 inch, and then place steak mixture in the center of each foil piece.

Bring the edges of foil together, and then seal the edges on each side by folding them, and then place the packets over the grilling rack.

Shut the grill and then cook for 10 minutes until steaks have cooked, turning halfway.

Uncover the packet, top cheese over the steak mixture, and then continue cooking for 2 minutes until the cheese melts.

Serve straight away with a bun.

Nutritional Information per Serving:

Calories: 520 Cal; Total Fat: 24 g; Saturated Fat: 10 g; Cholesterol: 76 mg; Carbohydrates: 38 g; Fiber: 2 g; Sugar: 13 g; Protein: 25 g;

Caprese

Yield: 4 packets, 1 packet per serving

Preparation Time: 10 minutes

Cooking Time: 20 minutes

Total Time: 30 minutes

Difficulty: Level 1

MAIN INGREDIENTS:

- 2 large tomatoes
- 4 chicken breasts, about 6 ounces, skinless
- ¼ teaspoon salt
- ¼ teaspoon ground black pepper
- ½ teaspoon Italian seasoning
- ¼ cup basil pesto
- 8 ounces sliced mozzarella cheese

DIRECTIONS:

Set the grill, and then let it preheat at medium-high heat setting.

Meanwhile, cut each tomato into four slices, and then cut each slice in half.

Prepare the chicken and for this, make four crosswise slits into each chicken breast, about ¾-inch apart.

Cut out four pieces of aluminum foil, each piece about 18-by-12 inch and then place chicken in the center of each foil piece.

Spoon 1 teaspoon of pesto into each slit of chicken, place ½ slice of tomato and a cheese slice in each slit.

Sprinkle salt, black pepper, and Italian seasoning over the chicken breasts, bring the edges of foil together, and then seal the edges on each side by folding them and then place the packets over the grilling rack.

Shut the grill and then cook for 20 minutes until the chicken has cooked, turning halfway.

Serve straight away.

Nutritional Information per Serving:

Calories: 430 Cal; Total Fat: 24 g; Saturated Fat: 3 g; Cholesterol: 145 mg; Carbohydrates: 6 g; Fiber: 1 g; Sugar: 2 g; Protein: 49 g;

Pineapple Chicken

Yield: 4 packets, 1 packet per serving

Preparation Time: 10 minutes

Cooking Time: 15 minutes

Total Time: 25 minutes

MAIN INGREDIENTS:

- 4 chicken breasts, skinless
- 1 medium red bell pepper, cored, chopped
- 1 small white onion, peeled, chopped
- 1 medium green bell pepper, cored, chopped
- 1 can of pineapple pieces, about 15 ounces

For the Sauce:

- 1 cup teriyaki sauce
- 1 cup sesame dressing

DIRECTIONS:

Set the grill, and then let it preheat at medium-high heat setting.

Meanwhile, cut the chicken 1 ½ inch thick pieces, and set aside until required.

Pour the teriyaki sauce in a medium bowl, add sesame dressing, and then whisk until combined.

Cut out four pieces of aluminum foil, each piece about 18-by-12 inch, and then place chicken, pineapple, onion, and bell pepper pieces in the center of each foil piece.

Drizzle the sauce over the chicken and vegetable mixture breasts, bring the edges of foil together, and then seal the edges on each side by folding them and then place the packets over the grilling rack.

Shut the grill and then cook for 15 minutes until the chicken has cooked, turning halfway.

Serve straight away.

Nutritional Information per Serving:

Calories: 222 Cal; Total Fat: 7.1 g; Saturated Fat: 3.4 g; Cholesterol: 85 mg; Carbohydrates: 11 g; Fiber: 0.2 g; Sugar: 9.7 g; Protein: 27 g;

Grilled Apples

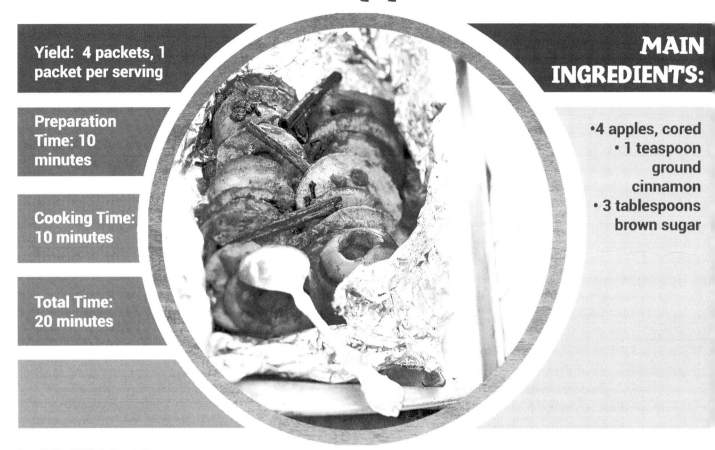

Yield: 4 packets, 1 packet per serving

Preparation Time: 10 minutes

Cooking Time: 10 minutes

Total Time: 20 minutes

MAIN INGREDIENTS:

- 4 apples, cored
- 1 teaspoon ground cinnamon
- 3 tablespoons brown sugar

DIRECTIONS:

Set the grill, and then let it preheat at medium heat setting.

Meanwhile, prepare the apples and for this, core them, and then cut the apples into wedges.

Cut out four pieces of aluminum foil, each piece about 8-by-8 inch, and then place apple wedges in the center of each foil piece.

Place cinnamon in a small bowl, stir in sugar, and then spoon the mixture over the apple wedges.

Bring the edges of foil together, and then seal the edges on each side by folding them and then place the packets over the grilling rack.

Cook the apples for 10 minutes until softened, and then serve straight away.

Nutritional Information per Serving:

Calories: 113.7 Cal; Total Fat: 0 g; Saturated Fat: 0 g; Cholesterol: 12 mg; Carbohydrates: 31 g; Fiber: 3 g; Sugar: 27.4 g; Protein: 0.5 g;

Chocolate Cherry Cake

Yield: 8 packets, 1 packet per serving

Preparation Time: 10 minutes

Cooking Time: 20 minutes

Total Time: 30 minutes

Difficulty: Level 1

MAIN INGREDIENTS:

- 1 can of cherry pie filling
- 1 box of brownie mix

DIRECTIONS:

Set the grill and then let it preheat at medium-high heat setting.

Meanwhile, place pie filling in a large bowl and then stir in brownie mix until combined.

Cut out sixteen pieces of aluminum foil, each piece about 12-by-12 inch, and then place ½ cup of the cake mixture in the center of eight foil pieces.

Cover the top of the cake filling with another piece of foil, fold the edge to seal the packet, and then place them on the grilling rack.

Shut the grill with its lid and then bake for 20 minutes, turning halfway.

When you are done, serve the cake with a scoop of ice cream.

Nutritional Information per Serving:

Calories: 117 Cal; Total Fat: 1 g; Saturated Fat: 0 g; Cholesterol: 0 mg; Carbohydrates: 27 g; Fiber: 1 g; Sugar: g; Protein: 1 g;

Chapter9: Kitchen Mathematics

For Volume/capacity:

US Measure	Imperial	Metric	
1 cu inch [in3]		=	16.387 cm3
1 cu foot [ft3]		=	0.02832 m3
1 fluid ounce	1.0408 UK fl oz	=	29.574 ml
1 pint (16 fl oz)	0.8327 UK pt	=	0.4732 liters
1 gallon (231 in3)	0.8327 UK gal	=	3.7854 liters

For Mass:

US or Imperial		Metric	
1 ounce [oz]	437.5 grain	=	28.35 g
1 pound [lb]	16 oz	=	0.4536 kg
1 stone	14 lb	=	6.3503 kg
1 hundredweight [cwt]	112 lb	=	50.802 kg
1 short ton (US)		=	0.9072 t
1 long ton (UK)		=	1.0160 t

Memorize the following measurements and you will be good
3 teaspoons=1 tablespoon
16 tablespoons=1 cup
16 onces=1 pound

For Temperature:
To convert from Celsius to Fahrenheit, $(0\,°C \times 9/5) + 32 = 32\,°F$
To convert from Fahrenheit to Celsius, $(32\,°F - 32) \times 5/9 = 0\,°C$

Chapter10: Index

K
Kale Smoothie

L
Lentil Soup
Lima Bean Stew
Lemon and Parmesan Broccoli
Lemon and Dijon Salmon
Lemon Garlic Shrimps

M
Mango and Banana Smoothie
Mashed Potato Pancakes
Meatloaf
Mushroom Sliders

P
Peach and Mango Smoothie
Peanut Butter Hummus
Peanut Butter Apple Rounds
Pepperoni Pizza
Pineapple and Yogurt Dip
Pineapple Chicken
Philly Cheesesteak
Popcorn Chicken
Popcorn Balls

Q
Quinoa, Cranberry, and Almond Granola
Quinoa Fritters
Quinoa Stuffed Mushrooms

R
Rainbow Fruit Kabobs

Ranch Chicken Tenders

S
Sandwich on Skewers
Shrimp Boil
Shrimp Fried Rice
Sloppy Joes
Southwest Couscous
Spinach Omelet
Spaghetti with Basil Pesto
Sriracha Honey Wings
Strawberry Soup
Strawberry Shortcake Smoothie
Sweet Potato Wedges
Sweet Potato and Black Bean Quesadilla

T
Tuna Salad Sandwich
Tomato Spaghetti
Tomato Soup

V
Vanilla Cupcakes
Vegetable Wraps
Vegetable Soup

W
Whole-Wheat Waffles

Y
Yogurt Bowl with Berries
Yogurt with Cereal and Bananas

Reference

5 Everyday Foods That Help Kids Grow Strong. (n.d.). Retrieved from https://www.healthy-height.com/blogs/growth-nutrition-guide/5-everyday-foods-that-help-kids-grow-strong

A. (2019a, August 25). Sweet Potato Wedges. Retrieved from https://www.healthylittlefoodies.com/sweet-potato-wedges/#wprm-recipe-container-4371

A. (2020a, May 3). Yogurt Breakfast Bowl Recipe. Retrieved from https://diethood.com/yogurt-breakfast-bowl/

Abraham, L. (2020, September 16). PB&J Sushi. Retrieved from https://www.delish.com/cooking/recipe-ideas/recipes/a56690/pbj-sushi-recipe/

All-Fruit Popsicles | Minimalist Baker Recipes. (2020, May 26). Retrieved from https://minimalistbaker.com/all-fruit-4-ingredient-popsicles/

Amanda @ .running with spoons. (2019, October 17). Black Forest Smoothie | running with spoons. Retrieved from https://www.runningwithspoons.com/black-forest-smoothie/#_a5y_p=4172515

Apples by the Fire. (2001, March 8). Retrieved from http://allrecipes.com/recipe/27184/apples-by-the-fire/?evt19=1

Avocado and Cheese Toasties | Simple Toddler Recipes. (n.d.). Retrieved from http://simpletoddlerrecipes.com/recipe/166/avocado-and-cheese-toasties/

Best Foods to Increase Height in Children. (n.d.). Retrieved from https://parenting.firstcry.com/articles/best-food-increase-height-children/

Black Bean & Corn Salad - Meatless Monday. (2020, April 15). Retrieved from https://www.mondaycampaigns.org/kids-cook-monday/recipes/black-bean-corn-salad

Black Bean Burgers - Meatless Monday. (2020, March 27). Retrieved from https://www.mondaycampaigns.org/kids-cook-monday/recipes/black-bean-burgers

Caprese Chicken Foil Packs. (2017, May 2). Retrieved from https://www.pillsbury.com/recipes/caprese-chicken-foil-packs/2ac1725a-72b9-4ff1-9337-1d8c809b5db0

Cheesy Quinoa Stuffed Mushrooms - Meatless Monday. (n.d.). Retrieved from https://www.mondaycampaigns.org/kids-cook-monday/recipes/cheesy-quinoa-stuffed-mushrooms

Chickpea, Avocado and Cucumber Salad - Meatless Monday. (2020, March 27). Retrieved from https://www.mondaycampaigns.org/kids-cook-monday/recipes/chickpea-avocado-and-cucumber-salad

Chickpea Salad Sandwiches - Meatless Monday. (2020, August 6). Retrieved from https://www.mondaycampaigns.org/kids-cook-monday/recipes/chickpea-salad-sandwiches

Chocolate and Lentil Protein Muffins. (n.d.). Retrieved from https://www.sarahremmer.com/flourless-chocolate-lentil-protein-muffins/

Chocolate Avocado Smoothie. (n.d.). Retrieved from https://www.mynourishedhome.com/chocolate-avocado-smoothie/

Chungah @ Damn Delicious. (2020, February 1). Shrimp Boil Foil Packets. Retrieved from https://damndelicious.net/2015/08/26/shrimp-boil-foil-packets/

Cinnamon Apple Chips. (n.d.). Retrieved from https://www.superhealthykids.com/recipes/homemade-cinnamon-apple-chips/

Classic Egg Salad Sandwiches Recipe. (n.d.). Retrieved from https://www.eggs.ca/recipes/classic-egg-salad-sandwiches

Classic Tomato Soup - Meatless Monday. (n.d.). Retrieved from https://www.mondaycampaigns.org/kids-cook-monday/recipes/classic-tomato-soup

Classic Tomato Spaghetti - Meatless Monday. (2020, May 21). Retrieved from https://www.mondaycampaigns.org/kids-cook-monday/recipes/classic-tomato-spaghetti

Classic Vanilla Cupcakes Recipe. (n.d.). Retrieved from https://www.eggs.ca/recipes/classic-vanilla-cupcakes

Curried lentil soup. (2019, October 1). Retrieved from https://tags.news.com.au/prod/newskey/generator. html?origin=https%3a%2f%2fwww.kidspot.com.au%2fkitchen%2frecipes%2fcurried-lentil-soup-recipe%2f85r cib4a&16013808941222380042

Davison, C. B. (2020, September 22). Cool Ranch Chicken Tenders. Retrieved from https://www.delish.com/ cooking/recipe-ideas/recipes/a47278/cool-ranch-chicken-tenders/

Donut Apples are Our Favorite Low-Cal Snack! (2020, September 22). Retrieved from https://www.delish. com/cooking/recipe-ideas/recipes/a52053/donut-apples-recipe/

E. (2008, April 1). One Minute Flax Muffin - Low Carb Recipe - Food.com. Retrieved from https://www.food. com/recipe/one-minute-flax-muffin-low-carb-295649

Easy Cinnamon Bun Popcorn. (2019, October 15). Retrieved from https://thebigmansworld.com/easy-cinnamon-bun-popcorn/

Flaxseed and Blueberry Oatmeal. (n.d.). Retrieved from https://www.littlebroken.com/wholesome-flaxseed-and-blueberry-oatmeal/

Flaxseed Raisin Bread. (n.d.). Retrieved from https://americanprofile.com/articles/flaxseed-raisin-bread-recipe/

Fried Egg & Bacon Breakfast Sandwich Recipe. (n.d.). Retrieved from https://www.eggs.ca/recipes/fried-egg-tomato-and-bacon-breakfast-sandwich

Fruit Kabobs. (n.d.). Retrieved from https://www.spendwithpennies.com/fruit-kabobs/

Fruit Salad with Kiwi, Strawberries, and Mango - Meatless Monday. (2020, April 13). Retrieved from https:// www.mondaycampaigns.org/kids-cook-monday/recipes/fruit-salad-with-kiwi-strawberries-and-mango

Funston, L. (2020a, September 16). Cheesy Baked Tacos Is The Coolest Way To Serve Tacos To A Crowd! Retrieved from https://www.delish.com/cooking/recipe-ideas/a50265/cheesy-baked-tacos-recipe/

Funston, L. (2020b, September 16). Philly Cheesesteak Foil Packs. Retrieved from https://www.delish.com/ cooking/recipe-ideas/recipes/a53182/philly-cheesesteak-foil-packs-recipe/

Green Smoothie. (n.d.). Retrieved from https://www.superhealthykids.com/recipes/how-to-make-a-green-smoothie/

Grilled Foil-Pack Cheesy Fries. (2019, May 3). Retrieved from https://www.pillsbury.com/recipes/grilled-foil-pack-cheesy-fries/8f4eeaad-9221-48be-bff6-a7dbe6210952

Grilled Vegetable Wraps with Creamy Coleslaw - Meatless Monday. (n.d.). Retrieved from https://www. mondaycampaigns.org/kids-cook-monday/recipes/grilled-vegetable-wraps-with-creamy-coleslaw

H, J. (2019, July 15). Foil Packet Chocolate Cherry Cake. Retrieved from https://www.coffeewithus3.com/ foil-packet-chocolate-cherry-cake/

Hard Boiled Eggs. (n.d.). Retrieved from https://www.eggs.ca/recipes/basic-hard-boiled-eggs

Healthy Foods For Growing Kids. (n.d.). Retrieved from https://www.healthxchange.sg/children/food-nutrition/healthy-food-growing-children

Herb and Cheese Omelet - Meatless Monday. (n.d.). Retrieved from https://www.mondaycampaigns.org/ kids-cook-monday/recipes/herb-cheese-omelet

How to Make a Great Grilled Cheese for Kids. (n.d.). Retrieved from https://www.verywellfit.com/how-to-make-a-grilled-cheese-sandwich-290305

J. (2020b, May 30). Shrimp Fried Rice Recipe. Retrieved from https://steamykitchen.com/1331-shrimp-fried-rice.html

J. (2020c, July 15). Lemon Garlic Foil Packet Shrimp. Retrieved from https://www.theroastedroot.net/ lemon-garlic-foil-packet-shrimp/

K. (2020d, July 12). Kid-Friendly Grilled Vegetables in Foil Packets. Retrieved from https://kevcooksplants. com/kid-friendly-grilled-vegetables-in-foil-packets/

Kid-Friendly Peanut Butter Hummus Is an Adult Favorite, Too. (n.d.). Retrieved from https://www. thespruceeats.com/peanut-butter-hummus-2355626

Kids Can Make Cheesy Eggs in the Hole. (n.d.). Retrieved from https://www.foodnetwork.com/recipes/food network-kitchen/kids-can-make-cheesy-eggs-in-the-hole-with-bacon-3362545

L. (2015, April 12). Easy 20 Minute Sloppy Joes with Hidden Veggies Recipe. Retrieved from https:// momsbistro.net/easy-20-minute-sloppy-joes-with-hidden-veggies-recipe/

Lemon-Parmesan Broccoli Foil Packs. (2017, May 2). Retrieved from https://www.pillsbury.com/recipes/

emon-parmesan-broccoli-foil-packs/ca97f443-e6c1-4c38-ad3c-4efbf11a388c

Lima Bean Stew - Meatless Monday. (2020, April 8). Retrieved from https://www.mondaycampaigns.org/kids-cook-monday/recipes/lima-bean-stew

M. (2019, June 25). Baked Kale Chips. Retrieved from https://www.healthylittlefoodies.com/baked-kale-chips/#wprm-recipe-container-6256

M. (2019b, October 14). Chocolate almond date balls...a delectably healthy snack. Retrieved from https://hemanylittlejoys.com/chocolate-almond-date-balls-a-delectably-healthy-snack/

M. (2020e, August 3). Kid Approved Chicken Salad - the Whole Smiths. Retrieved from https://www.hewholesmiths.com/back-school-lunches-simple-mills/

Meatloaf. (n.d.). Retrieved from https://campbrighton.com/foolproof-kid-friendly-super-delicious-meatloaf/

Mini Chicken Parm Sliders. (n.d.). Retrieved from https://sandersonfarms.com/recipes/mini-chicken-parm-sliders/

Mini Mushroom Sliders - Meatless Monday. (2020, March 30). Retrieved from https://www.mondaycampaigns.org/kids-cook-monday/recipes/mini-mushroom-sliders

Miyashiro, L. (2020a, September 16). PB&J Apples. Retrieved from https://www.delish.com/cooking/recipe-ideas/recipes/a57151/pbj-apples-recipe/

Miyashiro, L. (2020b, September 22). The Only Deviled Eggs Recipe You'll Ever Need. Retrieved from https://www.delish.com/cooking/recipe-ideas/a51851/classic-deviled-eggs-recipe/

Miyashiro, L. (2020c, September 22). This Baked Popcorn Chicken Will Make You Swear Off KFC Forever. Retrieved from https://www.delish.com/cooking/recipe-ideas/recipes/a50923/baked-popcorn-chicken-recipe/

Palanjian, A. (2019, March 20). Cheesy Rice, 4 Easy Ways with Veggies. Retrieved from https://www.yummytoddlerfood.com/recipes/dinner/cheesy-rice/

Palanjian, A. (2020a, August 20). 4-Ingredient Baked Chicken Meatballs. Retrieved from https://www.yummytoddlerfood.com/recipes/dinner/baked-chicken-meatballs/

Palanjian, A. (2020b, September 15). 10 Toddler Smoothies with Hidden-Veggies (Big Kids Will Love Too!). Retrieved from https://www.yummytoddlerfood.com/recipes/breakfast/toddler-smoothies-with-hidden-veggies/

Patwal, S. (2020, September 18). 11 Best Foods That Help Increase Height In Kids. Retrieved from https://www.momjunction.com/articles/foods-for-increasing-height-in-children_00121489/

Pineapple Chicken Foil Packets. (n.d.). Retrieved from https://www.lecremedelacrumb.com/grilled-pineapple-chicken-foil-packets/

Pineapple Greek Yogurt Dip - Meatless Monday. (2020, April 25). Retrieved from https://www.mondaycampaigns.org/kids-cook-monday/recipes/pineapple-greek-yogurt-dip

Quick and Easy Tuna Salad Sandwich for Kids of All Ages Recipe - Food.com. (n.d.). Retrieved from https://www.food.com/recipe/quick-and-easy-tuna-salad-sandwich-for-kids-of-all-ages-216839#activity-feed

Quick Morning Pizza Recipe. (n.d.). Retrieved from https://www.eggs.ca/recipes/quick-morning-pizza

Quinoa Cranberry-Almond Granola - Meatless Monday. (n.d.). Retrieved from https://www.mondaycampaigns.org/kids-cook-monday/recipes/quinoa-cranberry-almond-granola

Quinoa Fritters. (n.d.). Retrieved from https://wendypolisi.com/kid-friendly-quinoa-fritters/

S. (2006, August 2). Glazed Pears Recipe - Food.com. Retrieved from https://www.food.com/recipe/glazed-pears-180402

Seidman, D. (2020, September 23). Foil Pack Sriracha Honey Wings. Retrieved from https://www.delish.com/cooking/recipe-ideas/recipes/a43212/foil-pack-sriracha-honey-wings/

Simple Egg Wraps Recipe. (n.d.). Retrieved from https://www.eggs.ca/recipes/egg-wraps

Southwest Couscous - Meatless Monday. (2020, March 19). Retrieved from https://www.mondaycampaigns.org/kids-cook-monday/recipes/southwest-couscous

Spaghetti with Basil Pesto - Meatless Monday. (2020, March 19). Retrieved from https://www.mondaycampaigns.org/kids-cook-monday/recipes/spaghetti-basil-pesto

Spinach Omelette Recipe for Babies, Toddlers and Kids. (n.d.). Retrieved from https://gkfooddiary.com/spinach-omelette-recipe-babies-toddlers-kids/#wprm-recipe-container-13917

Stuffed French Toast with Strawberries and Banana. (n.d.). Retrieved from https://www.eggs.ca/recipes/stuffed-french-toast-with-strawberries-and-banana

Sweet Potato and Black Bean Quesadillas - Meatless Monday. (2020, April 10). Retrieved from https://www.mondaycampaigns.org/kids-cook-monday/recipes/sweet-potato-and-black-bean-quesadillas

Taste of Home Editors. (n.d.-a). Buttery Horseradish Corn on the Cob. Retrieved from https://www.tasteofhome.com/recipes/buttery-horseradish-corn-on-the-cob/

Taste of Home Editors. (n.d.-b). Grilled Green Beans. Retrieved from https://www.tasteofhome.com/recipes/grilled-green-beans/

Taste of Home Editors. (n.d.-c). Grilled Hash Browns. Retrieved from https://www.tasteofhome.com/recipes/grilled-hash-browns/

Taste of Home Editors. (n.d.-d). Lemon-Dijon Grilled Salmon Foil Packet. Retrieved from https://www.tasteofhome.com/recipes/lemon-dijon-grilled-salmon-foil-packet/

Taste of Home Editors. (n.d.-e). Summer Strawberry Soup. Retrieved from https://www.tasteofhome.com/recipes/summer-strawberry-soup/

Team, G. F. (2020, August 7). Mango & banana smoothie recipe - BBC Good Food. Retrieved from https://www.bbcgoodfood.com/recipes/mango-banana-smoothie

Tilapia. (n.d.). Retrieved from https://www.superhealthykids.com/recipes/tapping-tilapia/

V. (2018, March 1). Hot Cocoa Popcorn Balls. Retrieved from https://www.messforless.net/hot-cocoa-popcorn-balls/

Very Veggie Soup - Meatless Monday. (2020, April 10). Retrieved from https://www.mondaycampaigns.org/kids-cook-monday/recipes/veggie-soup

Weelicious. (2020, June 4). Mashed Potato Pancakes. Retrieved from https://weelicious.com/potato-cakes/

Whole Wheat Waffles. (n.d.). Retrieved from https://www.superhealthykids.com/recipes/best-ever-whole-wheat-waffles/

Yogurt with Cereal and Bananas. (n.d.). Retrieved from https://www.superhealthykids.com/recipes/yogurt-with-cereal-and-bananas/